Eugene Murray-Aaron

The Butterfly Hunters in the Caribbees

Eugene Murray-Aaron

The Butterfly Hunters in the Caribbees

ISBN/EAN: 9783743322486

Manufactured in Europe, USA, Canada, Australia, Japa

Cover: Foto ©ninafisch / pixelio.de

Manufactured and distributed by brebook publishing software (www.brebook.com)

Eugene Murray-Aaron

The Butterfly Hunters in the Caribbees

CONTENTS

CHAPTER I

THE START

PAGE

The Dawson Boys — An Unexpected Vacation — A Roving Naturalist — Plans for the Expedition — Down the Bay — Anticipations of Danger — Tales of Hardship — Climbing the Andes — In Daily Peril of Death — Alone on the Rio Negro 1

CHAPTER II

THE BAHAMAS

Sea Serpents — Inhabitants of the Deep Sea — "Hard aport! Danger ahead!" — Derelicts — The Bahamas — Nassau — First Tastes of Tropical Life — Mighty Trees — The First Butterfly Hunt — A Butterfly's Bath — Butterfly Athletes — The Marvels of the Microscopic World 14

CHAPTER III

DOWN IN A DIVING-BELL

Wondering Darkies — Who are Americans? — The Name of our Continent — The English Army — Professor Watson's Offer — A Philosophical Skipper — Native Incredulity — The Diving-Bell — The Diver's Sensations — On the Bottom of the Sea — Plant-like Animals — Sponge Fishers — Phosphorescence of the Sea — The Immensity of Animal Life 27

CHAPTER IV

THE FIRST CAMP

To Sea in an Open Craft — Nature of the Bahama Isles — Columbus's Inaccuracy — The Camper's Life — Putting up the Tent — An Ideal Cooking Outfit — A Lucky Find — Senses without a Head — An Evening with the Moths — A Strange Bait — Four-winged Topers — A Lurking Snake 45

CHAPTER V

COLUMBUS AND HIS LANDFALL

Foraging for Breakfast — Picking Oysters from Bushes — Wholesale Fishing — An Abandoned Garden — The Danger of Poisonous Pests — A Sumptuous Lunch — The Preservation of Insects — Flamingoes — Imaginative Historians — Columbus's Character — Which is the "Landfall"? — Indian Slavery — Columbus's Untruthfulness . 62

CHAPTER VI

THE DEVIL-FISH

In Camp again — Negro Honesty — The Geographical Sense — Marvellous Memories — Training the Memory — The Collector's Outfit — Comparative Abundance of Butterflies — Spanish Cedar — A Devil-fish at Home — A Three-hearted Monster — The Dreaded "Kraken" 83

CHAPTER VII

DOWN THE ISLANDS

Migrating Butterflies — Samana or Guanahani — A Tropical Downpour — Meeting Old Friends — An Island "Pooh-Bah" — Camping on Great Inagua — Pugnacious Ants — Insect Pests — Their Sense of Smell — The Use of the Antennæ 99

CHAPTER VIII

THE EARLY HOME OF THE FREEBOOTERS

A Mulatto Landlady — The Multitudes of Blacks — The Early Natives — The Buccaneers — National Hypocrisy — The True Discoverer — Late Views of Columbus — Ant Cows — Herders and Protectors of Caterpillars — Ants versus Wasps — An Alligator's Nest — Luring an Alligator — Full of Fight — Ho! for Haiti — Flying Machines and their Future 113

CHAPTER IX

THE BLACK REPUBLIC

A Glimpse at Haitian History — The Most Degraded Land in Christendom — A Study in Human Government — An Old Friend — Elisha — A Dark View of Haiti — Vaudoux Witchcraft — "Haiti," its Derivation and Spelling — A Creole Dinner — An Array of Fruit — "Matrimony" — A Pet Lizard 129

CHAPTER X

AN EARTHQUAKE

Gabe — Early Morning in the Tropics — Orchids and Air-plants — Water-cocoanuts — High Prices — The Ceaseless Tom-tom — A Native Dance — The "Sablier" or Sand-box Tree — Strange Noises — Zombies, Jumbies, and Duppies — The Need of Missionaries — A Terrible Moment — Earthquakes — Cap Haitien — "The Ill-fated City" — Toussaint l'Ouverture 145

CHAPTER XI

INTO THE WILDERNESS

The Palace of Sans Souci — The Citadel of La Terriere — Productiveness of the Land — Along the Coast — A Squalid Land — Port au Prince — A Paris of Mud — A Useful Lesson — The American Minister —

President Hippolyte — A Strong Contrast — Start of the Cavalcade — A Funeral Procession — Vaudoux Orgies — Snake Worship . . 163

CHAPTER XII

CAMP CONTENTMENT

Luxuriant Vegetation — The Cocoanut-palm — The Useful Bamboo — Gorgeous Butterflies — The Butterfly Gun — A Coveted Rarity — Ladder Building — The Moth Beacon — A Weird Sight — Giant Bats — *Loupgaroos* or Vampires — A Midnight Experience — A Rich Harvest — Humming-birds — A Tiny Songster — Scientific Names . 180

CHAPTER XIII

ABOVE THE CLOUDS

Anticipations — Mountain Heights — An Unattempted Feat — Difficult Moutaineering — An Ideal Camp — Harry's Description of a Mountain View — Planting the Flag — Frost in the Tropics — A Mountain Sunrise — The Inscription above the Clouds — Attacked by a Wild Boar — Excellent Marksmen — A Still More Luxuriant Wilderness — Cannibalism — American versus French Republicanism — Haitian Dignitaries 197

CHAPTER XIV

THE NEGRO'S PARADISE

Jamaica the Blest — Port Royal — A History of Guilt — The Earthquake's Vengeance — A Miraculous Escape — A Famous Hurricane — Pelicans — Quashie Lingo — Street Sights — The Jamaica Museum — Modified Negro Rule — Thoughts of Home — King's House — Sir Henry and Lady Blake — Luxuriance of Life in the Tropics — An Ideal Winter Resort — Troops in Cloudland — Chased by a Storm 215

CHAPTER XV

IN THE HOME OF HOMERUS

PAGE

Richard, the Driver — The Convicts — Rock Fort — Cane River Falls — The Scarcity of Whites — The Negro Races — The "Gordon Riots" — George William Gordon — The Carnage at Morant Bay — Terrible Retribution — Bath and its Attractions — Cacao, Coca, Coco, and Cocoa — "A *Homerus!* A *Homerus!*" — The Baths of Saint Thomas — A Romantic Legend 230

CHAPTER XVI

A MIDNIGHT HORROR

Hunting *Homerus* — Loathsome Bait — A Profitable Day — Cuna Cuna Pass — Ideal Roads — The Maroons — A Barbarous Execution — A Deserting Guide — Blood-curdling Sounds — A Lost Burro — The Valley of the Rio Grande — Wholesale Fruit Culture . . . 247

CHAPTER XVII

BACK TO THE FROZEN NORTH

Deceptive Clouds — A Comprehensive View — From Straw Hats to Ulsters — A Glad Home-coming — Mr. Dawson's Plans — The Doctor's Words of Praise — The Work at the Academy — A Proud Moment — A Well-earned Honor — A Handsome Balance — "Ho! for the Spanish Main!" 259

LIST OF ILLUSTRATIONS

The Doctor was already about twenty feet in the air, on a stout ladder — *Frontispiece*

PAGE

"Hard aport! Hard aport! A derelict on the port bow!" 18

Jumping into the small-boat, they were soon under the bell . . 38

They turned the box over, and a good-sized snapping-turtle fell out . . . 54

The Doctor's gun rang out, followed quickly by those of the boys . 72

As far as the eye could reach there extended a scattered column of butterflies 100

The crowd continued to grow even more frantic . . 178

Instantly their guns rang out sharp and in unison . 208

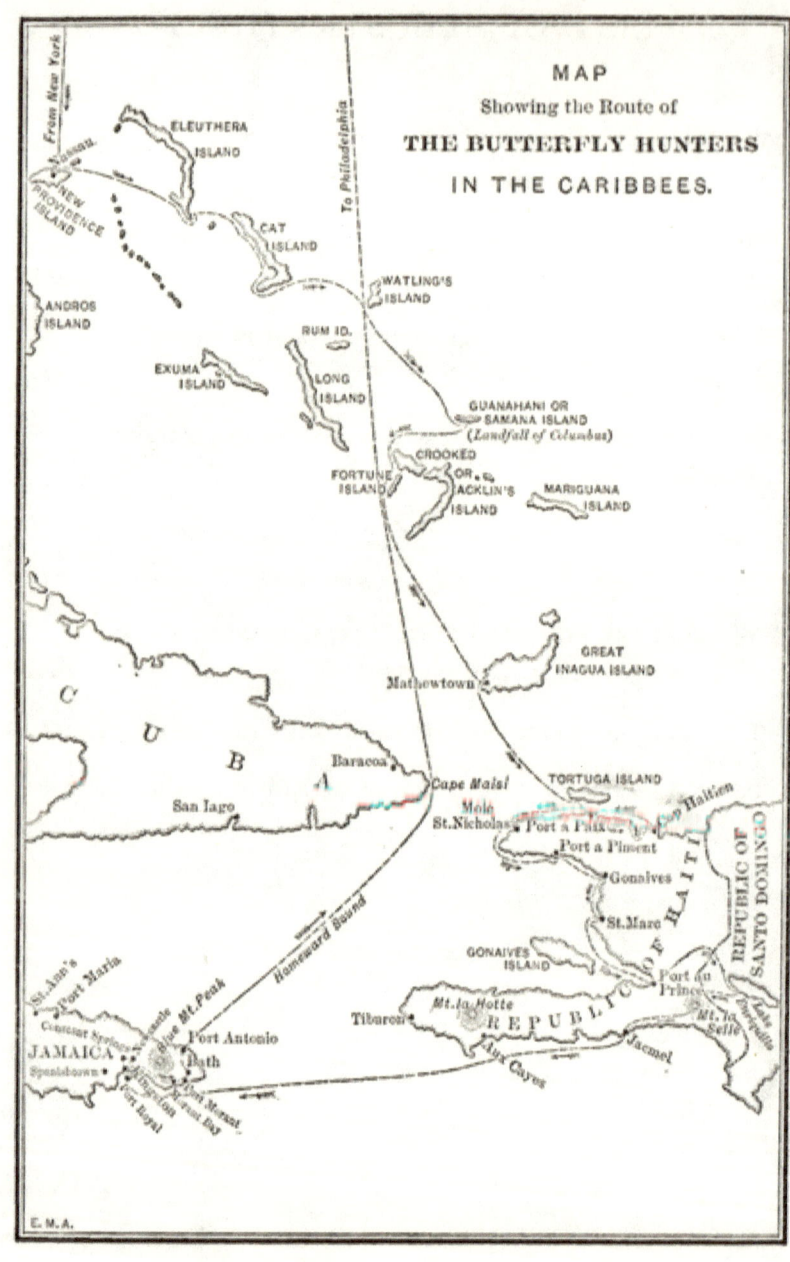

THE BUTTERFLY HUNTERS
IN THE CARIBBEES

CHAPTER I

THE START

The Dawson Boys — An Unexpected Vacation — A Roving Naturalist — Plans for the Expedition — Down the Bay — Anticipations of Danger — Tales of Hardship — Climbing the Andes — In Daily Peril of Death — Alone on the Rio Negro

AS the steamship "Orizaba" of the Ward Line swung out of its dock at the foot of Wall Street, New York, there were no more interested and excited spectators, either on shore or on deck, than two boys who eagerly hung over the rail of the departing vessel and watched everything with that sort of attention which showed plainly that it was all new to them. That these boys were brothers was easily told by their close resemblance; the older of the two was sixteen, the younger would be fourteen in a few weeks, yet so closely were they alike in appearance and in size that it would have been quite natural to take them for twins. Their eagerness in watching all that was going on about them — sailors running hurriedly here and there on the vessel with great ropes, while other ropes were being released on the wharf by the men stationed there, with over all the din and bustle the voice of the officer in charge shouting his orders,— was due to the fact that never before had they been on the deck of an ocean liner, nor even watched the departure of one of those monarchs of the sea.

Coming from an inland Pennsylvania town, Edward and Harry Dawson had had but little chance to become acquainted with the ways of old ocean. Once their father had brought them with him on one of his business trips, and had taken them for a few days to one of the seaside resorts; but beyond a short sail in the inlet, where some diminutive waves made them feel rather curious in the region of the stomach, they had had no experience with the heaving, uncertain sea. Now they were actually bound on a voyage that would take them far from land, and to that most romantic of all regions, the West Indies, to be gone as many weeks as it would take them to get a good idea of the peculiar life and wonderful natural conditions of that chain of islands.

When, soon after they had returned to their boarding-school for the fall term, they had been sent back by the principal with a letter to their father, stating that as scarlet fever had broken out in the school, it was thought best to close it until all danger had passed, and that it would probably be well on towards the new year before the school would open again, Mr. Dawson was at a loss to know just what to do with the boys. To such a practical, hard-working man of business it seemed a pity to have the boys idle for so long a time, just after they had had the benefits of the summer vacation. Mr. Dawson was a manufacturer of iron who by watchfulness of details had made himself a successful man, and who was now considered one of the wealthiest men in his part of the State. His own education had been derived from hard experience in earning his living from early boyhood, much more than from books or teachers; and this had made him firm in the intention to give his sons the best education which his very ample wealth made possible.

A day or two after the return of the boys from school, Mr. Dawson received from a friend of his earlier years a letter asking him whether he could not find the writer a position in his large mills as an accountant or in some other way help him to get a position. Dr. Richard Bartlett had had everything in the way of a finished education that his older friend, Albert Dawson, had wanted, but could not afford to take. In addition to an excellent college training his father had been able to give him the benefit of a medical education in Germany, after which he had been allowed to spend two or three years in travel in Europe and parts of Asia. But complete as was his knowledge of his profession, he was utterly unfit to follow it, because the idea of tying himself down to one locality had grown distasteful to him after so much travel, and he had not been back in his home very long before he accepted a position to go to South America for the museum of the university in Germany where he had been graduated.

From that time until the receipt of this letter Mr. Dawson had heard nothing of his friend. From the letter he learned that the Doctor had spent the last ten years in travelling in all sorts of out-of-the-way places, collecting museum material and writing books of travel. Now he hardly knew where to turn for a new country to visit and had about made up his mind that he would settle down for awhile in his own land, if he could get anything to do but "saw bones," as he called the practice of medicine. Quick to make up his mind, Mr. Dawson was but a short time in deciding that such a rover as his friend had been would be of but little value in an establishment like his; and he was equally quick to see that here was the very chance for his boys that he was looking for. After consulting his wife and getting her consent to his plans, he wrote a letter to his friend that quickly brought the Doctor to the Dawsons' home and which resulted, much to the delight of the boys, in the following plan.

As Ned and Harry were likely to have at least ten weeks that ought to be given to their education, but which must be spent away from school, it was decided that nothing could be better for them than a tour in the charge of Dr. Bartlett. Both of the boys had already shown marked fondness for the study of Natural History; together they had already made a very fair collection of the butterflies of their region, and had added to it some that they had got by exchanging with collectors in other parts of the country. Mr. Dawson was a firm believer in the wisdom of boys having a hobby of some kind, to fill up their idle moments, and to give them an object to strive after; and he had often had cause to notice what a benefit travel was to any one who went through the world with his eyes open. Therefore he was quick to avail himself of this chance for his boys, for he was anxious that they should have a taste of the delights of travel; and he was delighted to find that this would be possible under the charge of so thorough a student of Nature, and such an experienced traveller.

The Doctor knew so well just what would be wanted on such a journey, and he was so thoroughly conversant with all the countries which it was proposed they should visit, that Mr. Dawson was quite willing to leave all the details to him, with such advice as the boys' mother had to offer. It took but a little time to get together all that was needed for the trip, and their start was delayed but a few days; almost before they had been able to realize that they were really to visit a region, the wonders of which they had read of with the utmost interest, they were afloat.

Now they stood on the deck of the "Orizaba," waving good-bye to their father, mother, and little sister, until the steamer, having reached the mid-stream, wheeled around and started down the river on her majestic way. As the faces of the dear ones faded away, the boys were joined at the rail by the Doctor, who understood the importance of taking their attention with other things so that the realization of the fact that they were going so far from home might not cause home-sickness, which he knew would come soon enough. Beginning with the mighty Brooklyn Bridge, on down past the Statue of Liberty, and so out into the broader Bay, there was plenty to see and to talk about to chain their attention, and the boys had already learned that their companion of the voyage was a prince among entertainers. The great fund of knowledge that he had brought back from his many tours over the world and the easy way in which he told anything made an impression on the boys from the first, and they naturally turned to him for any desired information.

Neither Ned nor Harry was a boy that was likely to stand at the head of his classes either in recitations or in conduct; yet both were likely to make as much out of the information that they brought from school as any of their companions. There are many boys like them who have excellent memories and good eyes that are always open to observe anything that is worth knowing, who are not quick to tell what they know to their teachers or their fellows. The Doctor had the ability to an unusual degree to draw out of such boys the information that they had on any subject, and add his own to it in such a way that the boys hardly realized that they were undergoing an examination and at the same time receiving instruction. This it was that Mr. Dawson believed would make the Doctor an excellent guide for the boys, for he foresaw that they would come home laden with a wealth of valuable and entertaining information which they would have gained without having the feeling that it was being pumped into them.

"Doctor," said Ned, as they still stood looking towards the fast disappearing New Jersey shore, "why couldn't we just as well have gone to Florida by train and then across to the Bahama Islands by steamer? Wouldn't that way have been quicker, and wouldn't we have escaped going around Cape Hatteras, where you told us the other day it was sometimes so dangerous?"

"As Florida and the Bahamas produce much the same sort of things for exporting to other countries, neither of them has much that the other needs, and, therefore, there is no call for a steam line between them. There are sailing-vessels that go between the two at irregular times and make such ports as are most convenient, but the only way to go from one to the other by steam is by New York as we are doing. Hatteras has an ugly way of tossing vessels around, but just at this season of the year we are not likely to have any trouble with it. We are rather late to catch the tail-end of any West Indian hurricanes or the equinoctial storm of the third week in September, and we shall probably get back in time to escape the severe storms of the early winter."

"Well, even if we don't get caught in any bad storms at sea," broke in Harry, "we are likely to have some pretty tough times on land before we get back, aren't we?"

"If by tough times you mean such experiences as Stanley tells us of in his accounts of African explorations, Harry, you are very likely to be disappointed. All the countries that we are going to are fairly well civilized so far as dangers from wild beasts or wild men are concerned. We may have some strange and rather uncomfortable experiences if we camp out in Haiti, as I expect we shall, but that we shall meet any real dangers, where lives are at risk, is most unlikely, simply because I have brought you young men out to see the world and go home to use the information that you have got, and not to run the risk of having you killed."

"But, Doctor," said Harry, whose ideas of adventure were not at all satisfied by such a tame outlook as this, "can't we cut short some part of the trip so as to have a little time for visiting wilder regions?"

"I hardly think that will be necessary; there are a good many little hardships to contend with of which you yet have no idea. It is the little worries that often are the most difficult to stand, and it may be that an accumulation of these may be too much for both of you, and you may be glad to turn your faces homeward before you have finished the trip."

"Doctor," said Ned, "you must have had a lot of dangerous adventures. Tell us some of them."

"Perhaps I have not had such thrilling experiences as you want to hear about," the Doctor replied, looking at his watch; "but as it is more than an hour before supper time we can sit down over there on the port side, and I will tell you some of the things that have happened to others, and perhaps some of my own experiences.

"It is a mistake commonly made to think that the hardships encountered by explorers in the far north are greater than those that they are likely to have to endure in tropical countries," began the Doctor, when they were seated. "I have tried the upper Yukon, in Alaska, and the far north of Siberia, and it has always been my experience that it was much easier to battle against the cold and the effects of poor food — the two principal hardships in Arctic regions — than to put up with the many troubles besetting the traveller in warm countries. Insect pests alone are quite equal to all that is to be endured in the frozen north. And when it comes to tropical fevers, of which there never seems any end, so many kinds are there, the difficulties of life in some parts of those regions are more serious than can be put into words.

"But you boys want to hear about other sorts of hardships. Of the sort that you are interested in perhaps there are none that are of a more serious nature than those incident to mountain-climbing, where great heights are to be overcome. The efforts of Edward Whymper in the Andes of Ecuador and Peru are among the most remarkable in that direction, for Mr. Whymper has the ability to stand such exposures to a great degree, and he has made the science of mountain-climbing a study for many years. He spent 212 days in the upper regions of the Andes, and of that time 204 nights were spent at elevations of over 8000 feet, or over one mile higher than the highest mountain in the State of Pennsylvania. During thirty-six nights he slept above the 14,000 feet line; during eighteen he was from about 16,000 to 17,500; and on one night he camped at an elevation of 19,500 feet. At this height he was above the highest land in North America and was for many hours at a point where most men would find it difficult to live for more than an hour or two.

"These extreme heights had to be reached on foot, for no mule or horse can long live there, and many of their Indian carriers had to abandon their bundles and return to lower levels because of the 'mountain sickness,' that made its appearance among them. Finally, on the 4th of January, 1880, he and several of his party reached the crowning peak of Chimborazo, at an extreme elevation of 20,498 feet, thus accomplishing what had been tried by many explorers, among them the great Von Humboldt, but which had never before been done. At such heights as this, and at much less in the case of most men, breathing becomes very difficult, the lungs act with a gasping motion instead of with their regular method of taking in the air, almost unbearable headache and considerable fever are constant, and an overpowering feeling that one is incurably ill, are the principal symptoms.

"If the explorer has either a weak heart or lungs, he is sure to discover it long before he reaches such excessive heights, by bleeding at the mouth and nose and in extreme cases, by fainting fits that are Nature's ways of warning him that unless he quickly descends to lower levels, he has not long to stay on this earth. Greater heights than these have been reached in the Himalayas of India by Messrs. Graham and Boss, who ascended Mt. Kaben to the 23,700 feet line, and by Mr. Conway, who recently climbed the highest peak of the Mustagh Range to almost as great an elevation; but it is doubtful, when the rough climate of the upper Andes is considered, whether any of the others underwent as great hardships as did Mr. Whymper and his party.

"There is another form of hardship that is, perhaps, even more trying to courage and endurance, and that is the life among hostile natives, where their hatred for whites makes it necessary for the explorer to adopt their dress and customs and in every way hide the fact that he is of the Caucasian race. One explorer, whom I met in Tunis, had just returned from an exploration of the interior of Morocco, where the Mohammedan hatred for those from Christian lands is such that they will not allow them to enter their territory. At the hourly risk of his life this daring explorer had dyed his hair and skin so as exactly to represent a Turk, and then, in the company of a half-grown boy whose father's life he had saved, and whom he knew he could depend upon as a guide, he had gone into the interior as a wandering beggar. As he could not hope to escape detection when speaking their language, which he understood imperfectly, he was represented by his guide as both deaf and dumb, from exposure to the desert's heat when a child.

"Thus these two journeyed for many weeks, both running constant risk of suspicion, discovery, and death; the one bravely asking the way and begging alms from settlement to settlement, and the other keeping his eyes wide open and charging his memory with countless facts never before observed by a white man. Afterwards he told me that he would not go through such an experience again for many thousands of dollars; but when I asked whether he would not if by so doing he could add as much to scientific knowledge as he had by the trip just finished, he promptly answered that he would gladly do so. It is that sort of stuff that the true explorer is made of, boys. There is a wide gap between the unostentatious and painstaking explorer, who cares everything for facts that will be of lasting value to his fellow-men, — such men as were Livingstone in Africa, and Bates on the Amazon, — and those so-called explorers to whom the good of their fellows is not of as much importance as the money that comes from lectures and books about their paltry work."

"What was the worst experience you ever had, Doctor?" Ned asked.

"Oh, I have usually taken too good care of my skin to get into any scrape that would compare with those that have fallen to the lot of others. So far as I now recollect, the most disheartening time in all my travels was when I awoke one morning on the headwaters of the Rio Negro in Brazil, to find that my Indian carriers had disappeared, and with them had gone all of my belongings. To wake up suddenly to a realization of the fact that I was entirely alone in an unknown wilderness, with every scrap of my food gone, my guns and ammunition stolen, even such oilcloths as I would need in a rain missing, was for a while so terrible that my conviction was firm that nothing but death was before me. It is one thing to contemplate death, but quite another to sit calmly down to wait for its coming, and I soon found myself planning how I could get out of the wilderness alive. So far as I could judge it ought to be about eighty to one hundred miles to the nearest settlement. It did not take me a great while to find some drifted logs that had been cast up by the last high water, and, as you will soon find out, Nature in the Tropics provides all the rope-like materials that are needed in the shape of lianes or 'vegetable ropes,' as we call them.

"I spent the first day in tying together a raft, only stopping long enough to find some wild guavas and other small fruits to keep off the pangs of hunger. On this sort of a rude raft I managed to paddle myself down stream for six days, without seeing a soul and with only wild fruits to keep me from absolute starvation, although I felt pretty near that when at last I did sight a native village. There I found a Mameluco in charge of the town, who was a very intelligent man. The runaways who had treated me so badly had attempted to sell my outfit in this village, and he had at once seen that the things were only such as a white was likely to own, and that they must have been stolen. Therefore, he detained the men until he could find out how they had come by such valuable belongings. Taking fright at his firmness and knowing that if they were found out they would be severely punished, they managed to escape in the night and take with them some of the stolen things, but were obliged to leave behind those most valuable to me. Though it is said that 'all's well that ends well,' I shall never look back on those days, alone in that mighty wilderness, without a shudder."

CHAPTER II

THE BAHAMAS

Sea Serpents — Inhabitants of the Deep Sea — "Hard aport! Danger ahead!" — Derelicts — The Bahamas — Nassau — First Tastes of Tropical Life — Mighty Trees — The First Butterfly Hunt — A Butterfly's Bath — Butterfly Athletes — The Marvels of the Microscopic World

AFTER supper the boys took up their positions on each side of the Doctor and clamored for more stories of adventure; but the Doctor was not inclined to tell any more stories just then, preferring to learn something from his young companions. From Harry he got the information that they were then passing the New Jersey coast, which was principally noted for its seashore resorts.

"And mosquitos and sea serpents," broke in Ned.

"There aren't any sea serpents, are there, Doctor?" asked the younger boy.

"Nothing concerning the animal world has given rise to more differences of opinion among those who ought to know than this question that you have asked me," was the reply. "In my opinion there is such a thing as a sea serpent, although I have never seen one. But I have met so many truthful men who assured me that they had seen such a monster, that I cannot refuse to accept their combined testimony. Now, too, since the naturalist Gosse has written so much in proof of the existence of such reptiles in the deep sea, scientists are beginning to change their views, and there are many of them who firmly believe in these creatures. That they are true serpents may be doubted, but that some descendants of strange monsters of an earlier age are yet dwelling in the least travelled portions of the southern oceans is most likely.

"No doubt the stories sometimes told of great serpents seen along the South American and African coasts are largely based on the fact that the high floods of the rainy seasons wash the large land serpents out to sea. As some of these are known to be over thirty-five feet long, it is not strange that some wonderful lengths are reported, when we remember that they are usually seen but for a few moments, and that the imagination may easily lead the unscientific observer into mistakes. However, there have been accurate reports made by several naturalists in late years who have seen and sketched these creatures, and there seems to be the best of reason for believing that there are some very strange animal forms in the ocean that have not yet been classified by naturalists."

"Can either of you tell me some of the peculiarities of the animal life that exists under us in the depths of the sea?" the Doctor suddenly asked, after all had remained quiet for awhile.

"Most that are brought up from great depths are without eyes, I have read; and many are of the most beautiful colors," Ned answered.

"The fish near the top of the ocean never go very deep, and those that live on the bottom never come very high up, so there are two sorts of animals in the sea; and where it is very deep there is a space in which there is hardly any life, if any at all," added Harry.

"All that is quite correct," commented the Doctor. "It is based on many facts found out by expeditions sent by this country and England. The lack of eyes is due to the fact that light cannot penetrate to a very great depth, and they do not need eyes, for Nature seldom supplies what there is no need for. Another strange thing about the deepest forms is, that as they must dwell where a great weight of water, due to its depth, is constantly pressing on them from all sides, they withstand the pressure just as we do that of the air in which we live. But as this makes it necessary for them to have a very considerable internal pressure that is equal to that which they have to withstand, naturalists on bringing them to the surface often witness the strange sight of their bursting as soon as they get to the upper air."

"Who started this work of finding what was on the bottom of the ocean?" asked Harry.

"The engineers of the first ocean cable, who found it necessary to get a better idea of the bottom of the seas, on which those long iron ropes were to rest; and in that way the first facts regarding the wonderful life of the ocean bottoms was brought to light."

The principal part of the next day was spent by the boys and Doctor Bartlett in a thorough examination of the machinery and methods in use on the ship. In the chief engineer they found not only a man who was thoroughly versed in the science of his calling, but one who took much delight in imparting his knowledge to such interested and attentive listeners as he found the boys to be. From the boiler and its pumps to the electric lighting arrangements and the powerful search-light at the bow, everything under his care was made as plain as need be. So, too, with the second officer, into whose care they were given by the captain; they found him to be one who could not take too much trouble to explain all the many riggings and odd appliances over which he had charge.

Naturally both boys looked forward to the approach of Cape Hatteras with some dread. For the first two days they had felt nothing of seasickness save slight uneasiness after the rather heavy meals which the appetizing sea air made necessary. But the cape was passed while they were safely asleep in their berths, and when they awoke in the morning it was in the smooth waters that intervene after the Gulf Stream has been passed and the Bahama Sea is being approached. This was a delightful surprise to them, and they were inclined to take the Doctor to task for frightening them unnecessarily.

That night, after a day spent in studying the geography of the land that they were first to visit, they were about ready to turn in again, when the voice of the officer on the lookout rang out suddenly and loud:—

"Hard aport! Hard aport! A derelict on the port bow!"

Every one who was yet on deck rushed to the port side of the vessel, and the boys reached there, without in the least knowing what was the great attraction, just in time to see the "Orizaba" rush past what to them appeared to be a half-sunken raft with its centre rounded up.

"What was that, Doctor? what is a derelict?" asked Ned.

"A derelict is a vessel, or a part of one, or even a large part of its cargo, that has been wrecked and abandoned at sea, and is moving about at the will of the currents, without any one knowing just where it is likely to turn up next. The one we just passed did not look very dangerous, but in fact it was of the most dangerous kind. It was a vessel of some size, probably a three-masted schooner, which, entirely overturned in some severe storm, is now drifting around bottom side up. As the cargo is still in it, and it is filled with water, it is very nearly as heavy as the water and, therefore, shows only a small part above the surface. The most watchful lookout is likely to overlook such a hulk as that at night, and no eyes can by any possibility see it on a dark night. Yet there is so much of the water-soaked bulk under the surface that, if we had run into it, strong as this vessel is, we might quite well have sustained such injuries as would have made it the work of the most skilful sailor to take us into the nearest port safely.

"It is a fair estimate to say that there are in all oceans over three hundred such dangerous craft, drifting idly from point to point. Our government and that of Great Britain are both active in searching for these vessels, and, where they can be, they are brought into port, but more frequently they are blown into pieces with dynamite. The reports for the last year show that 1086 vessels were

"HARD APORT! HARD APORT! A DERELICT ON THE PORT BOW!"

them much higher than some oaks at home, but the size of the trunk and the way the main roots started away from the trunk above ground was quite different from any growth that they had seen in northern woods. So far above the ground did these buttresses start and so far did they reach out before they disappeared in the earth, that, as Ned said, it would have been quite possible to stable a horse between two of them.

"Doctor," asked Harry, "shall we see any bigger trees than this one?"

"Yes; we shall see some that go far beyond this both in height and in expanse. Probably the tallest trees are the giant Sequoias of California, of which you have read and seen pictures, although there are a few in the interior of Australia that are about their equals. In Jamaica we shall see some royal specimens of the Banyan trees, or Sacred Figs of India, as they are often called. They will be of such expanse that this tree would be quite lost in comparison. It is the Banyan, I am inclined to think, that Milton alludes to in his 'Paradise Lost' as the tree from which was made the fig-leaf clothing that was first worn in the Garden of Eden. Perhaps the most celebrated of those vegetable monsters is one that I have had the pleasure of swinging my hammock under in India. As you know, the great size of the Banyan trees is due to their throwing their branches to some length and then sending others down to the ground, which take root and virtually make other supporting stems. In this way the tree at last comes to look like a vast collection of trees, all growing closely together, but an examination soon shows that it is all one growth and has its origin in one main trunk which is often from ten to fifteen feet through. The famous Indian tree has more than one thousand of these smaller trunks supporting the immense weight of the whole growth, under which fully five thousand men could comfortably stand at one time. It is believed with good reason that it is over two thousand years old, and is not unnaturally worshipped by the superstitious natives, not as a god itself, but as a tree in which many gods must have found shelter when they were visiting this earth."

On the morning of their second day in the Island of New Providence the boys were introduced to their first butterfly hunt in the tropics. With their nets and boxes they all took an early start for a garden on the outskirts of the town, where the Doctor had procured the right to catch all that they could of their coveted treasures, and there they had the great joy of seeing at the first moment a species that was entirely different from anything they had yet seen. The Doctor, who had caught butterflies in almost every part of the world, was much amused at the enthusiasm with which they ran after species which they would in a little time be looking upon with utter indifference because of their abundance. But he said nothing of this sort, for he well knew the joy of such work in new fields, and he did not intend that anything should take from their intense enjoyment of all the newness around them. That butterfly collecting was quite a different thing in this much hotter sunlight the boys soon found out to their sorrow, and Ned was the first to come to the

Doctor with the remark that he had not supposed that it could be so hot in October, even though the sun was so much more directly overhead. At this the Doctor laughed, saying:—

"Why, my boy, this is delightfully cool weather as compared with what you would experience if you were to go down to the Isthmus of Panama or the Island of Trinidad. There you would find the thermometer above 115 degrees in the sun oftener than not. Fortunately from this on you will become more and more accustomed to such high temperature, and before you realize it you will think the present heat nothing whatever. Then, too, you will have, wherever you go, cool nights, when sleep will always be comfortable and refreshing."

Just then Harry came up in a hurry, with a look of wonder in his eyes and with a beautiful green and black butterfly in his hand.

"Now don't laugh at me and say that I am dreaming, but if I didn't find this butterfly in the water over there, actually bathing, then I don't know how to tell the truth."

"Well, I felt some headache from the hot sun," retorted Ned, "but I had no idea that it was hot enough to affect Harry's mind so soon. Next thing he will be finding them taking athletic exercise or learning to play football."

"Oh, you can poke all the fun you want to, Ned; but I really saw this beauty sitting at the edge of the water, and every few moments walking a little way into it and shaking its wings and legs just as though it was trying to throw the water over itself. What could it have been doing such a queer thing for, do you think, Doctor?"

"Harry's description of what he saw is a very good one, and the butterfly's motive I think I can make plain if you will give it to me." So saying the Doctor took the insect and carefully examined it under the magnifying glass which he always carried in his pocket.

"Yes, it is as I thought," handing both the butterfly and the glass to Harry. "At the roots of the wings and on the upper part of the body you will see a lot of little reddish specks, which under the glass you will see are nothing else than very tiny eight-legged insects of the family of mites or ticks. These are what is termed parasitic on the butterfly; that is they are living on it and getting their nourishment much as a tick or a flea gets it from us — by sucking the blood. Of course this causes the butterfly much the same sort of annoyance that the flea causes us, and therefore it was with the intention of getting rid of these pests by drowning them that the little beauty was doing such an un-butterfly-like thing as taking a bath."

"Well, I guess the joke is on me this time," said Ned, with a laugh.

"It was not alone your laughing remark about bathing butterflies that showed that you had no idea how many queer habits the little creatures have," the Doctor commented. "What you have said about their taking athletic exercise was also somewhat at fault. Many butterflies have the habit of sitting for a long time in one position and then suddenly darting off into the air, rushing around a few times in a circle without any apparent motive, resuming their former position and sitting as quietly as though they had not just been indulging in a sort of romp all alone. What but the desire to take exercise or to show their wonderful powers of wing to some mate who is hidden in the foliage near by can account for such a performance, no naturalist can say; and it is generally accepted that they are taking exercise."

"Don't you think, Doctor, that there is just as much that is interesting in the ways of the insects, as there is in the bigger world?" Harry asked.

"Far more, in my opinion; there are more different kinds of insects and insect-like creatures described by naturalists than there are of all other animal life together and of all flowering plants added. Of the beetles alone there are nearly 11,000 different kinds found in the United States, and it has been estimated that when naturalists are done with the classification of the wasps, ants, and bees, and their tribe, they will find not less than 35,000 different sorts in South America, and perhaps as much as 150,000 in the entire world. But it is when we begin to make our investigations with the microscope that we get our first just ideas of how many and minute are the works of Dame Nature in the world of little things.

"As compared with the common house-fly, the elephant is a mighty monster, yet he is no bigger in comparison than the fly is when compared with some of the little objects found living upon the latter. More than a dozen different creatures are found living within the body of the fly and getting sustenance from his food or blood. In his proboscis there is often to be found coiled up a tiny, hair-like worm, that causes the poor fly much inconvenience and sometimes results in his death. So, too, in the tiny digestive organs of the smallest mosquito may be found two kinds of little parasites that live there perfectly content to let their host do the food-getting while they ride around inside all their lives, getting their food without any trouble but to eat it. The wonderfully big and grand universe that the telescope reveals to us in the unthinkable distances of space is no more marvellous in its way than are the creatures of the tiny worlds that the microscope divulges to those who will use it with care and patience."

CHAPTER III

DOWN IN A DIVING-BELL

Wondering Darkies — Who are Americans? — The Name of our Continent — The English Army — Professor Watson's Offer — A Philosophical Skipper — Native Incredulity — The Diving-Bell — The Diver's Sensations — On the Bottom of the Sea — Plant-like Animals — Sponge Fishers — Phosphorescence of the Sea — The Immensity of Animal Life

WHEREVER our party went in or around the town they were followed by a throng of the youngsters of the region, in whose faces awe and curiosity were strangely mixed. The words "duppy-bat catching" were used by them in stage whispers from time to time, and at last Harry asked the Doctor what they meant by the expression.

"Duppies are the harmless spirits of this part of negroland, and to them signify about what you boys used to understand by brownies and fairies. There is something so unreal about butterflies to these ignorant people that duppy-bat exactly expresses their ideas of them. You will find that the smaller children are afraid of butterflies although they show but little dislike for a cockroach or a big, savage-looking beetle."

"There is another thing I notice," said Ned; "when any of these people speak of us, they call us Americans, just as if they were not as much Americans as we are. Why is that?"

"Although the name America is geographically applied to all the Western World, from which the name first came, still from this time on you will hear it used as only applying to that part of the New World which is within the boundaries of the United States. These people around us consider themselves Bahamans, not Americans. And so you will find it everywhere; we will meet Haitians, Jamaicans, Nicaraguans, Venezuelans, and so on, but never Americans unless we run across some one from our own land."

"Just now you spoke of the part of the New World from which the name America came. Wasn't the name taken from that of Amerigo Vespucci, the discoverer?"

"That is the statement that you will find in most geographies and histories so far as I know them. The word is one that has never been found in any document published in Europe prior to the time of the discovery, but it is one that was found by the early discoverers in two places here: once in the Veragua region where it still is in use as the name of a locality; and again, in Nicaragua, where it was in use as 'Amerrique,' to signify a mountain chain and a powerful Indian tribe. On a map made in October, 1502, which is entitled 'A nautical chart of the islands newly found in the regions of India,' and which was made by Cantino, and is believed to have been corrected by Vespucci himself, the name first appears as 'Tamarique,' which was a shortening of the words *terra Amarique*, or the land of Amerique."

"Wasn't it a very strange thing that this tribe should have a name so like that of the discoverer?"

"There again we have little proof of the accuracy of the theory that has been so long taught. That Amerigo spelled his name in different ways there is the best of proof; and that he did not spell it so as to resemble that of the Indian tribe until that name was given to the land is well shown by more than one of his signatures. All that can be said at this late day is that the name was far more likely to be given to the land in honor of the principal tribe that dwelt in the neighborhood that was first so named than in honor of a then obscure voyager, who was not even in command of the expedition that made the discoveries in that region."

In Nassau the boys were treated to their first sight of the English army; for wherever there is an English colony, there must also be that upholder of Her Majesty's power and dignity, the wearer of the red coat. The Doctor was anxious for them to be impressed with the splendid condition of these troops, because the next military display that they would see would be in Haiti, and he knew that they would enjoy the farce there presented, all the more from being familiar with the perfections of the English troops. While they were there, the Governor, Sir Ambrose Shea, on whom they had called with a letter of introduction, reviewed the troops, and our party were invited. Then they were able to admire, in all their glory, the well-drilled men in their beautiful and showy uniforms. Turning from the sight of this splendor to the Doctor, Harry said : —

"Why can't our government, which is called the richest in the world, afford to dress its soldiers so they will look so handsome? Just think how miserable they would look by the side of these scarlet coats and white trousers in their dusty gray-blue uniforms!"

"Which would you rather wear," asked the Doctor, "if you were in an open field or a thicket, and were under fire? Is the man in the red or the one in the dull blue most likely to be a good target for the guns of the enemy? And there is another peculiarity which adds both beauty and danger to the uniform. It is the way in which the leather strap and the polished Queen's arms are worn across the breast. Any one who will take careful aim at that shining ornament on the breast is quite sure to inflict a deadly wound, as the most dangerous part of the whole body to shoot into is thus plainly marked out."

On the fourth day of their stay at Nassau the Doctor arranged a treat for the boys that was their first real experience of adventure and was ahead of anything promised them. This was nothing less than a chance to go down in a diver's bell after coral and other sea growth, in charge of an experienced diver. There was there at that time an expedition from an American museum provided with a complete diver's outfit, and one of the party was well acquainted with such work. Doctor Bartlett was well known by reputation to these gentlemen, and he took the boys to examine the treasures that they had collected. Many were the expressions of wonder and admiration that these called forth, but over nothing did they show more admiration than over the many odd creatures that the diving expert had collected from the bay.

"I never had any idea how beautiful and queerly shaped these things were. And I didn't think there were so many different kinds in one part of the world."

So said Ned, but Harry, always the more practical of the two, added:—

"Couldn't we get some of these near shore, just by diving? We are both good divers and can swim all day."

"There are rather too many sharks in these waters for me to let you run that risk, my boy; but for a few pennies we can get any number of the little darkies of the town to dive for us, and while I will not vouch for the condition that the things that they bring us will be in, still I think it will be worth while to give it a trial."

"If the young men want to have a taste of the sort of life the diver lives, it would be perfectly convenient for me to take one at a time with me to-morrow in my bell, if you are willing, Doctor, to entrust them to my care," the collector of these things, Professor Watson, offered.

"I have tried that sort of thing myself," the Doctor replied, "and I know it to be perfectly safe. If the boys want to try the experiment, I have no objection whatever."

Where is there a healthy boy who would not jump at such a chance, just as Ned and Hal did? It took but little time to arrange that they were to be at the harbor ready for a morning's sail at an early hour so that the outgoing tide might be in their favor.

The boat used by the student of sea life was not much to look at nor much for fast sailing; but, as that gentleman said, it was as steady as a tub, and steadiness was what was wanted for the sort of work that he was doing. The skipper of this boat was what the Professor called an African brunette; in other words, he was as black and shiny as a negro's skin can ever get. But under the black skin and the rather fat face without much expression in it there was a lot of common sense which made him a perfect master of his boat, and which also made his conversation by no means the least enjoyable of the morning's experiences.

"Hi! but hit do beat the massy what do breng all you 'Mericans out here in dis brilin' sun to go down after dese debilments in de water. Long as dey was just de Pr'fesser what wanted dem, I spected dat he was a little wrong in his head. But now, when all dese yuther 'Mericans come out after de same tings, dey yaint no use atellin' me dat dey yaint o' some use in de way o' doctorin', or fo' some kind o' charms."

"Our friend here," the Professor remarked, with a laugh, "is much disturbed on this subject. That men, sane men, can possibly care to spend time and money in studying these things simply for the sake of the naturalist's love of discovery, without any idea of turning their work towards its money value, if it have such, he will not believe. That there is some hidden motive that induces me to go to all this trouble under the sea, he feels sure. In this he is not so very different from many in our own country, for the question, 'What good is it?' is perhaps the one of all others that we naturalists have to answer most frequently; do we not, Doctor?"

"Everywhere that I have been," was the reply, "I have found that it was well-nigh impossible to get natives to understand that the things that are the most desirable treasures to us are simply of use, in most cases, for the study of their forms, habits, and distribution, with the intention of arranging them according to our ideas of the whole plan of Nature. One of the hardest customers of this sort that I have yet met I came across in our own State of Pennsylvania. He was a blacksmith in the interior of Pike County, which is a forsaken wilderness from one end to the other. The old fellow was an ardent trout fisherman, and it was in one of his wanderings after the speckled beauties that he came across the place where I was encamped. He had evidently been watching me from a distance for some time as I stood near a stream catching dragonflies, or, as they are there called, 'snake-feeders.'

"At last he stepped out of the bushes and asked me if he might inquire what use I made of these insects; and I could see by his half-contemptuous manner that he expected me to admit that I wanted them for fish bait, and that I was not skilful enough to get along without live bait. He could not be made to understand that the simple study of their peculiarities could be of any interest to me; and when I attempted to explain to him that there were some among those that I had collected that were not yet even named, he delivered me such a lecture as I am not likely to forget for many a long day. He reminded me that in the days of the Garden of Eden all animals had been called together by Adam and had then received names. According to his reasoning Adam was the only man who had been given the right to give names to the animals, and, as he had no doubt given these creatures names, it was my duty to find out and use only them. He ended by saying that if I caught all the snake-feeders, as he called them, the snakes would die for want of food, and I had no right thus to interfere with the plan that had been devised for feeding them.

"It was no use for me to try to explain to him that in using the name 'snake-feeder' he was using a name not given by Adam; nor was it possible for me to get him to believe that the dragonflies had really nothing to do with feeding the snakes. With the parting warning that in all probability I would be severely stung by my stingless captives, he left me to my own wicked ways, as he believed them to be. So you see one does not have to go very far from home to meet people who have the oddest ideas on the subject of naturalists and their habits."

While this conversation had been in progress, the diving ground had been reached, and already the Professor had made such arrangements as were necessary to lower the diving-bell from the bow of the boat. The bell, an iron concern, much the shape of a water glass upside down, was so fastened at the bowsprit with rigging that it was possible to let it down or raise it up rapidly or slowly at will and according to signals given by its occupant to those on deck. Professor Watson explained how fresh air was supplied by an air-pump on deck and how the impure air was allowed to escape, showed how substantially everything about it was made, and how safe from accidents it was likely to be, and then said:—

"You young men must not think that going down in a

diving-bell is absolutely painless, but at the same time the pain is quite unimportant. Soon after the bell begins to sink, you will feel some pain in the ears and over the eyes, which will continue until the bottom has been reached. Then it will disappear to be replaced by a feeling of depression, such as we have from a headache on a damp, murky day; but it will come back again when we start to rise, and will continue until we reach the surface again, when it will disappear in exchange for a delightful feeling of buoyancy and comfort. I often think it is worth while to make such a descent just to realize how delightful life in the pure, bracing air really is, and how much I have to be thankful for that submarine diving is not my occupation, but only my recreation."

"Professor, what causes the pain you speak of?" asked Ned, who had been chosen to go down first, and who was putting on a pair of swimming-trousers preparatory to climbing into the bell, which already was swinging over the water.

"Although our bell will go down very gradually, not faster than four feet a minute, or at the rate of a mile in twenty-two hours, our heads are not able to adapt themselves to the change in air pressure which follows from the increasing depth. Of course you understand that the bell acts just as does a tumbler when placed in water upside down. The air in it cannot escape and, being very elastic, it is much condensed by the pressure of the non-elastic water. The bell as it goes down has the air within it condensed into a smaller space, until at thirty-three feet under the surface it is forced to half its former bulk, and the bell will be half full of water, provided a greater pressure is not supplied by the air-pump on deck. Now the air as it grows denser presses on the outside of our bodies, but the channels through which it gets to the cavities in our heads are so small, as a rule, that there is at once an inequality in the pressure which bears upon certain nerves and causes this pain.

"Take the pain in the ears, for example: at once the increased pressure is felt on the tympanic membrane or 'drum' of the ear, but the change cannot be felt so soon on the other side of this membrane, because the air that reaches the inner ear passes through the narrow, crooked passages of the Eustachian tubes which communicate with the throat and nose and supply but a small amount of air at a time. Hence, while a change is going on in the air's density, it is felt instantly without, and but slowly within, and the inequality of pressure so caused gives rise to pain."

"How far can men go down in these bells safely, Professor?"

"There is an authentic record of one who went down and stayed several hours at the depth of two hundred feet, where the ordinary pressure of fifteen pounds per square inch had been replaced by one of eighty-seven pounds; but such a feat is most hazardous. Even one hundred feet may be considered unsafe for most men; only such as are young and blessed with perfect health, well regulated hearts, and strong lungs, can stay long at such depths. Bridge and harbor workers, at such depths, are frequently partially paralyzed, but they usually recover in a few days, and feel no further ill effects, if they do not return to the work.

"But you need have no feelings of uneasiness to-day, for we shall not go over twenty-five or thirty feet, at the most, and neither of you will suffer at that depth, once you are down," the Professor added, seeing a shade of apprehension on Ned's face.

"How well can we see down there?" Harry asked.

"With the water as beautifully clear as it is in this harbor, famed the world over for that very thing, fifteen feet will seem like a dark rainy day, and the depth to which we are going will be no worse than twilight or a moonlight night. However, that we may not overlook any treasures, I always keep two powerful bull's-eye lanterns in the bell, which I use for final examination. But as flame consumes the oxygen which we need for breathing, I burn the lanterns as little as possible."

By this time the Professor and Ned were ready for their downward trip, and, jumping into the small-boat which had been brought along, and was now fastened at the bow of the yacht, they were soon under the bell and had climbed into it. When all was ready, the boat was pulled to one side, and slowly the bell began to descend, while Ned within shouted to his brother strangely muffled remarks about the wonders he proposed bringing up with him. The work of directing the lowering and of keeping the air-pump under the right pressure was entrusted to an assistant, without whose aid the Professor never made a descent. Just as the edge of the bell was reaching the water, Ned's bare toes were seen waving beneath the rim, as the only way of expressing a good-bye handshake.

It would be hard to say to which of the boys the time passed the most deceptively: to Harry eager for the thirty minutes to speed by and bring his turn for submarine exploration, and to whom his watch appeared to go backward; or to Ned, charmed with the wealth of the wonderland he found so new to him, to whom the half-hour seemed hardly ten minutes, so soon was it gone. The latter, when again he stood on deck, was a picture of animation and eagerness, so bubbling over was he with all that he had seen and learned. But to all of Hal's questions he replied with a shake of his head.

"No, no; I promised the Professor I would not say a word about it, for it's only fair for you to have the fun of discovery, just as I did. My! Doctor, but I am glad you wouldn't tell us anything about what to expect, last night! Finding it all out this way is much better."

Naturally under these circumstances, Harry was most eager to start on the bottomward trip, and it was not long ere his bare foot was waving a farewell to those on deck. On the return of the bell and its passengers for the second time it was noon, and the Professor and Hal found a bountiful if rather primitive spread of sandwiches awaiting them under an awning that kept off the rays of the sun. It was planned that each of the boys should have another submarine trip during the afternoon, and therefore during the meal and for an hour or so afterwards while they all lolled about on deck and the crew were shifting the yacht to a new position, they had plenty of

JUMPING INTO THE SMALL BOAT THEY WERE SOON UNDER THE BELL.

time for an exchange of experiences and the asking of questions.

"Well, Ned, what most impressed you at the bottom of the bay?" asked the Doctor.

"The wonderful amount of strange life of every kind, I think. I had no idea that these things were so close together. I mean, I thought it was like a farm, where one part has one thing growing and another something else; I didn't know that it was so much like a woods where everything grew thickly together. Why, if different seas differ as much in their animals and vegetables as do different countries on shore, there must be millions of wonders under the ocean."

"They differ even more, in the opinion of naturalists," answered the Professor. "Von Humboldt, the great German explorer and scientist, has said that the sea contains in its bosom an exuberance of life of which no other portion of the globe could give us any idea. And Louis Figuier, one of the most delightful of French authors, says, that 'the inhabitants of the water are much more numerous than those of the solid earth.'"

"And what seemed most wonderful to you, Harry?" queried the Doctor.

"What Ned thought most surprising seemed so to me; next to that I think that those animal-plants that we brought up were the strangest discovery. I had seen them in collections, but I didn't know that they grew fast to things, and yet were really animals. What is the name you told me for them, Professor?"

"Zoöphytes, a name which is compounded from two Greek words meaning animal and plant. The name is not intended to show doubt in scientific minds as to whether they are of the animal or vegetable kingdom, although for many years this was a disputed point among naturalists. It is well known now that they are animals pure and simple; and the name only calls attention to certain peculiarities wherein they closely resemble the plant life with which we are most familiar. For instance, they divide themselves by offshoots as do some plants — the banana, for example; they are often crowned with bright colored organs much resembling flowers; and they are frequently rooted to one spot and wave about in the currents as do our flowers in the air."

"Do you always use the bell in your work?" asked the Doctor.

"No; I frequently use the diving-suit with helmet, of which I have two now on board. But, of course, they would not fit either of the boys, and I always prefer the bell when I can get company. Two pairs of eyes are much less likely to overlook anything in a small space, especially if one pair is as keen to observe as those belonging to these young men. Then, too, in these tropical regions I feel safer in a bell. Beside the sharks and an occasional sword-fish, there are several rather savage large fish hereabout, of which the *barraconta* is the worst, which might do a diver much harm. An acquaintance of mine was exploring some coral reefs at the southern end of Florida, when a *barraconta* severed the pipe that supplied him with air, and before he was brought to the surface in his heavy togs he was a pretty badly frightened man."

"Isn't the bell just as good as the suit, beside being safer?" asked Ned.

"It is possible to get around and examine a region more completely in a short time with the suit, but the bell is better for close study in one particular spot. Then in exerting any force, like moving a stone or using a hammer and chisel to loosen anything from a rock, the bell affords a much better 'purchase,' as it is called. A man sent down in a diver's suit to make repairs to a wharf, wishing to bore a hole, must be tied fast to something immovable before he can exert pressure sufficient to drive the auger into the wood. Otherwise, when he pushes against the auger, he simply floats away in the water."

After a good siesta, a rest from labor after the noontide meal, that is much needed and universally taken wherever the tropic sun pours down its heat, the Professor and Ned again "went below," to use a sea-faring phrase.

On their return Ned bounced out of the bell into the small-boat, saying:—

"Oh! Hal, what do you think? I found a little sort of spongy creature, which the Professor thinks is new to naturalists; and if it is, it will need a new name, and he says he will name it Edwardia, after me, its discoverer!"

"Gracious, I guess I'll have to look pretty sharp after lumps of jelly, too, if I don't want to be left behind," said Hal, after examining the queer little unshapen thing which Ned brought him to examine.

Lumps of jelly, as Hal called them, were neither so common nor so easily found as to enable him to discover another kind; and as the Professor explained after the bell had come up for the last time, and Harry had also found some fine, perhaps the finest specimens of the new species, such a discovery was now a rare occurrence, so he would give credit to both the young submarine divers by calling the species Dawsonia, if he found after study that it required a new name.

The labor of sorting and cleaning, labelling and bottling, with which the boys insisted on helping, was so considerable that the short tropical twilight was on them before they had reached the harbor. On the way in they overhauled and passed some native sponge fishermen who were bound for the town, and Ned asked:—

"Do these fellows collect sponges with a diving-bell, Professor, and are the sponges found here of the best kind?"

"Much of the collecting is done here, as it has been in India and Syria before historic times, by divers who go down without any apparatus, but who by long practice have become so expert that they can refrain from breathing under water two and even three minutes, and in that time can gather an armful of sponges. The Bahama sponges are rather hard and somewhat unyielding; the Syrian bring the highest prices, and those found here come about fifth or sixth in the scale."

As they drew near the wharves, and it grew darker, the whole harbor around them took on a most beautiful lustre and glistening sheen, one moment flashing forth little rays of ruby light, then pale green, then dark blue, and so throughout the whole scale of the rainbow.

"Look at the water, Doctor; what in the world makes it so beautiful?" asked Harry.

"That is what is called the phosphoresence of the sea, because in a way it reminds one of the dull glow of phosphorus after dark. The Professor can best explain it to you."

"It is the best possible answer to the question you asked me in the diving-bell this morning, Edward, when you wanted to know whether the ocean world was supplied with minute life as was the fresh water and the land," said the Professor. "The beautiful effect which you now see, and which you will see everywhere in the Tropics and, at certain seasons, in the northern waters, is produced by millions upon millions of minute animals known as *infusoria*. The commonest form of them, called *Noctiluca*, the 'night light,' is a round, jelly-like mass, scarcely more than one one-hundredth of an inch in diameter and with one long thread-like stalk which it uses as a leg, an oar, or a rudder, as best suits its purpose. All through their tiny bodies they have little light-giving points, which appear and disappear with great rapidity, giving forth the series of diamond-like flashes, the effect of which you now see. It takes about 25,000 of them to produce this effect in one cubic foot of water, and, therefore, a square mile of this bay, if they are but one foot deep in the water, must contain no less than 69,696,000,000 of these tiny light-givers. Yet, as a fact, the bay is probably filled with them down to its deepest point, and they may extend for hundreds of miles out to sea."

"Sixty-nine billions of lamps to the square mile! Well, that's an awful lot, but I must confess that I don't quite know how much it really is," said Ned.

"The way to deal with such big amounts is to reduce them to some easily understood comparison," the Professor rejoined. "If you could count at the rate of two hundred per minute, and keep it going for ten hours a day for every day except Sundays and holidays, you would yet be counting away at that number if you had started at the time of the birth of Christ. If one always remembers that at that rapid rate of counting, 12,000 an hour, 120,000 a day, and 36,000,000 per year, will be the result, it is always easier to get a just idea of the vastness of all stupenduous sums."

"Well, that sort of thing makes my head swim," Harry commented. "I never can stand much arithmetic; but that doesn't spoil my interest in the wonderful little creatures that cause this changeable color on the water. It is another fact to make us boys understand what a terrible quantity of living things there are in this world of which the most of us never have a thought."

"Yes," the Doctor said, as he turned on the wharf which they had now reached, to shake hands with the Professor; "we can well echo the words of the old Greek philosopher who said that 'there is nothing so small to the view but that it may become great by reflection.' And for a better understanding of that, boys, we have to thank Professor Watson, who has given us a day of enjoyment that it will be hard to equal anywhere on our trip."

CHAPTER IV

THE FIRST CAMP

To Sea in an Open Craft — Nature of the Bahama Isles — Columbus's Inaccuracy — The Camper's Life — Putting up the Tent — An Ideal Cooking Outfit — A Lucky Find — Senses without a Head — An Evening with the Moths — A Strange Bait — Four-winged Topers — A Lurking Snake

AFTER a few days more at Nassau, mostly spent in collecting butterflies and other insects, Dr. Bartlett announced that he had made arrangements with a trader who was bound on a trip among the islands in a small sloop, to take the young naturalists and their guide with him, touching at Watlings, Fortune, Great Inagua, Tortuga, and other of the islands in turn. So after a day given to packing for the trip, expressing some of their belongings on to await them at Jamaica, and a box or two of trophies homeward bound, with a few visits of farewells to new-found friends, they were up and ready for an early start on the next morning.

The craft which was now to be their carrier was in great contrast with the staunch and shapely ship "Orizaba," in which they made the first stage of their trip. It was of only about seventy-five tons' burden, and a crew of five men besides the skipper was quite sufficient to manage it. Some of these, as there were to be passengers in the cabin, where there were berths for but six people, would have to sleep on deck; but as they were all as black as

Guinea darkies ever got to be, that was no hardship to them. As the season had arrived when dry weather and moderate winds prevailed, and as their trip, for the most part, was to be through the sheltered channel between the islands, there was not much to fear in the way of a rough passage. The Doctor told them that while such small boats often did much more pitching and tossing in a heavy sea, they rode over the waves instead of "nosing" through them, and, consequently, were usually in less danger than a more pretentious vessel.

"Doctor," said Ned, as the distant city began to fade from their view, "how is it the biggest city of these islands is on one of the smallest of them?"

"Nassau is not only the principal city, but it is the only one in all these islands," was the reply; "and it is where it is, simply because it is the only safe deep-water harbor throughout the entire group. Naturally the seat of power in a colony must, if possible, be so located that the war-vessels of the home country can sail in and aid in suppressing rebellion; Nassau is at the only point where that is possible, not more than nine feet of safe water being in any other Bahaman harbor.

"The Bahamas, although they number over 1200 separate islands or keys, have a total area of only 3021 square miles, or only about two and one-half square miles, on an average, to each island, — not a very big farm in some of our Western States. They are throughout of one formation or origin; are of what the geologist calls calcareous rock, made from coral and shell hardened into limestone by the joint action of the water and air. There is nowhere any trace of volcanic action or upheaval, as there is everywhere else in the West Indies, but the whole is but one chain of monuments to the industry of the tiny coral animals. This stone, hard as granite in time, is sufficiently soft to be cut with a saw when at first exposed to the air. You saw them building with the white 'coquina' stone in Nassau, and cutting it into shape with ordinary hand saws; that was the Bahama rock as first obtained from the quarries. In a little while it hardens from exposure to the air, and in time becomes a hard and durable building-stone."

"Aren't there any mountains or volcanoes in the Bahamas?"

"No; the highest land is but 230 feet above the sea, or less than one-fourth the height of the Eiffel Tower in Paris, and is but a sand-heap due to action of the wind. Nor is there, outside of one island, Andros, running water."

The first landing was made at the southern end of the Island of Eleuthera, and, as the trader wished to sail around the island and make stops at several points, which would take him nearly two days, the Doctor decided that it would be as well for his party to land and make their first acquaintance with a camper's life. After finding a good opening in the coral reef through which a boat could safely make a landing, they loaded their camping outfit, a small provision supply, and their hunting material into the small-boat, and were safely rowed ashore by two of the crew. The point of their landing was a low, uninteresting, sandy shore, with stunted vegetation and a generally barren, deserted appearance.

It was only the middle of the afternoon when they

landed, and the boys wanted to go off at once on an exploring tramp; but the Doctor told them that it was always the better part of wisdom to make camp first, after which they would be quite independent. His

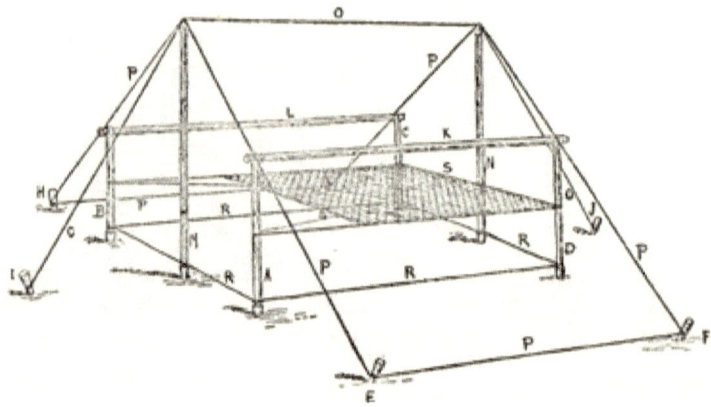

knowledge of camp life had enabled him to select, while in New York, a very complete camper's outfit, yet one that to the boys seemed surprisingly small. As he explained to them that it was always of first importance to provide shelter from wind and rain, they first directed their attention to unpacking and putting up their tent. This they were surprised, on unrolling it, to find consisted of nothing but several large rubber cloth blankets, a lot of clothes-line, ten heavy, sharp-pointed, hollow iron stakes, about thirty inches long, and two hand-axes.

"Where are the poles, Doctor? We've forgotten them," said Harry.

"There is a wholesale supply of them right over there in the undergrowth," was the reply, "and I'll appoint you,

Hal, a committee of one to get us four corner posts four feet long and as thick as your forearm. And you, Ned, may take the other hand-axe and cut two poles ten feet long, and two eight feet, and all about two inches thick; while I stay here and lay out the plan on the ground and place the stakes."

When, in less than a half-hour, the boys returned, they found that the Doctor had placed four of the iron stakes in the ground, as shown in the illustration, at the corners of a square (ABCD), with ten feet sides. Five feet beyond each of these, and in line with two of the sides, he had placed four other stakes (EFGH), and other marks on the sand showed that he was simply waiting for the return of the boys to drive these stakes in as far as they would go and set up the poles. Finding that they had selected these very well, he drove the four corner stakes almost to their heads in the ground. Then, taking the four short posts that Harry had brought, he trimmed them so that they would drive firmly into the tapering holes in the iron stakes, and they stood firmly in place. Across the top of two sets of these he placed the two ten-feet poles (K, L) that Ned had brought, notching them so that they fitted in place. Then, having driven the other four stakes in very firmly, he drove the remaining two stakes (I, J) five feet away from the other sides of the square, but opposite the middle instead of the corners.

Taking the two eight-feet poles that Ned had cut (M, N), he stood them upright between the corner stakes and in line with the two stakes last driven, and told the boys to hold them so. To one of these last stakes (I) he attached a piece of the clothes-line (O), and passing it tightly over the top of each of these upright poles, he carried it down to the other stake (J) and tied it, after drawing it as taut as possible. Then, starting at one of the four outside stakes (E), he fastened a piece of the rope (P), passed over the nearest corner post (A), up and across the eight-feet centre upright (M), down over the opposite corner post (B) to the outer stake in line (H); turning here at right-angles, he carried the line to the next outer stake (G), then again at right angles, up over a corner post (C) and the other eight-feet upright (N) and down to the next corner post (D) and outer stake (F), where the last turn at right angles carried the rope back to the point of starting (E). After it was firmly tied, he split open the strands of the rope on one side, passed a stick about two feet long between them and twisted it around until it seemed that if he drew the rope any tighter the outer stakes must pop out of the ground. But as they had been driven with their tops pointing outwards they remained firm, and the four corner posts and two eight-feet uprights were practically immovable, so firmly were they held by this manner of cording.

Now, to the intense interest of the boys, the tent frame assumed its shape, and they were able to anticipate the rest of the work when they saw that the rubber blankets were in three parts and provided with strings along their edges to tie them in place. The biggest of these was a monster, it seemed, when spread out, — ten feet wide and twenty feet long. This they drew over the cord last tied in place (P), until it hung by the middle over the first cord (O) that passed across the tops of the eight-feet centre uprights, with each side hanging over the pole across the tops of the corner posts. To the bottom of the latter, all the way around the square, a cord (R) was tightly drawn, and to this the strings on the end of the blanket were tied, and thus the roof and two walls were completed in one piece. The front and back walls, being of just the right size to fit those ends, were soon tied in place to the top and bottom cords (P and R), and then the edges of the roof were tied down over them so as to make a tight joint and keep out rain. In one of these end pieces there was a flap, which constituted the door, and, of course, this was the front of their rapidly built house.

Before the sides were finally tied in place, however, while it was still less difficult to move around within, the Doctor unrolled another bundle, from which he took three pillows, three large and very thick blankets, and what appeared to be a piece of strong fish-netting (S), ten feet long and six feet wide. This was firmly bound with rope, and at each corner, and about every fifteen inches along three of its sides, had strong iron rings. Through these the Doctor passed another rope (T), after he had laid the netting on the floor of the tent, with one of its ten-feet sides along the back wall, taking care to pass the rope around the outside of the corner posts and into notches which he had told the boys to cut about two feet from the ground. Then by passing a stick through the strands of the rope, as already described, he drew this netting so tight that the corner posts fairly groaned with the strain. This gave them a sacking, or bed bottom, at the back of the tent, six by ten feet in extent, allowing each one of them a space quite the size of an ordinary cot-bed. The edge of it towards the front made a very good settee, and there was a space left that was quite large enough for them to stand up in if need be, and plenty of room under the bed to stow their other outfits.

When all was finished, Ned remarked: —

"Why, Doctor, you must expect a terrible storm to-night, the way this is all tied together, and everything is staked fast."

"No, my boy, I do not expect anything of the sort, but I thought it was better for you to learn how to put this tent together in the firmest possible way while you had plenty of time and pleasant weather to do it in. I know how hard it is to hurry fast enough at such work when a storm is coming up, when every one understands his work, and I don't want to be caught that way some day with neither of you acquainted with the work. To-night we would, judging by the clouds and the time of year, have been quite safe in rolling up in our blankets on the dry sand, or in throwing together a rough shed of poles and thatch-palm leaves."

"Can't campers make a good, strong shelter in that way? I have often read about that as the way followed by hunters and explorers."

"Yes and no," was the reply. "If you are in a dense wood, or on the safe side of a hill, where a high wind cannot reach you, such a tent will do; but even such a roped-down covering as this we have here is sorely tried in a very heavy wind, and a severe West Indian hurricane would tear it all to tatters. But it is as safe as anything that can be made, holding its own against a violent tornado better than a frame house will, owing to the yielding nature of the rope braces."

Having provided themselves with shelter and beds for the night, the next task, the Doctor told them, was to unpack the cooking-outfit and prepare a meal. As the boys said, it did not seem as if the little oblong sheet-iron box, only eighteen inches long, and a foot wide, and a foot high, could possibly hold all that was required for a camper's kitchen. But when they saw it unpacked, and saw how every inch of its space had been utilized, they realized that it was quite sufficient to contain all that they could possibly need. The box itself was tin-lined, and was made to be used as a clothes-boiler in case any washing had to be done in camp. In one end of it was fitted a nest of square iron pans, fitting one in the other, and at the other a nest of round copper saucepans with detachable handles. A square canister held all manner of spices, flavorings, seasonings, baking-powder, soap powder, etc.; while another had a complete outfit of such medicines and accessories as the ordinary ailments called for. A large tin cup was the nest in which four others of decreasing sizes lodged, while a coffee-pot of ample size held a little alcohol lamp for use in cases of emergency. Knives, forks, spoons, toasting and broiling irons, a strainer, and a host of smaller articles too numerous to mention, completed this wonderfully complete and compact cook's outfit.

By the time this unpacking was finished it was nearly five o'clock, and the Doctor said that, as they did not need to begin to cook supper for a half-hour yet, the boys could hunt around a little while, while he gathered some dry drift wood for the fire. The boys, eager to see what was beyond them around the point of the island, started in that direction at a brisk walk. But they had not gone long, for the Doctor had not more than gathered enough firewood, before he heard Harry's voice calling : —

"See here, Doctor, what we have found. Isn't this good to eat?" At the same time both the boys came towards him as hastily as they could carry a large canned tomato box between them. The Doctor, thinking that they had found a box that had been lost overboard by some passing steamer and that it might yet contain one or two cans, was inclined to smile at their eagerness until he got a look at its contents, when he was much surprised and delighted.

"Hello, boys; that's a first-class find, and just in time to make us a delightful meal," he said, as they turned the box over, and a good-sized snapping-turtle fell out, which no sooner felt the sand under it than it put off for the water.

Ned jumped in front of their escaping dinner and turned him over on his back quickly with his foot, while the Doctor picked up one of the hand-axes and at one blow cut its head off. When the Doctor turned the creature over it started, much to their surprise, at once for the water again, although the head had been off several minutes, and even when it was carried some paces further inland and put down pointing towards the interior, it quickly turned about and headed for the water.

THEY TURNED THE BOX OVER AND A GOOD-SIZED SNAPPING-TURTLE FELL OUT.

"How can the poor creature go on living without a head, and how does it know with its ears, nose, and eyes gone, where the water is? I didn't know that such a thing was possible," said Ned.

"In all reptiles and their cousins, the frogs, lizards, and the turtle kind, there is a remarkable amount of vitality, life, and muscular activity, often remaining for several hours after the brain is severed from the body. What you have just seen is not unusual, and even more remarkable displays of this power have been observed of some of the lizard tribe. But such experiments are cruel and can only be excused on the plea of getting necessary food." So saying, the Doctor passed a knife into the still living turtle in such a way as to pierce the heart, and in an instant its struggles were over.

The Doctor then showed the boys how to clean and cut up the turtle, from which he extracted several pounds of clear, rich meat, while Ned was cleaning out and washing the upper shell under his directions. The latter was then placed on the edge of the undergrowth where it was sure to attract the attention of passing ants, which, the Doctor explained, were the best cleaners and scourers that could be employed for the purpose.

"Well, boys," the Doctor exclaimed, as the rich, appetizing odor of the stewing snapper made itself known to them, "this was a streak of good fortune, sure enough. Do you know that there are hundreds of people in New York to-night who would gladly give a five-dollar bill for that panful of stewed snapper? I had no idea that we should begin our camping experience in such a luxurious way, or I would not have brought those cans of prepared soup and potted game."

After they had made a hearty meal and had sat resting and talking for an hour in the gathering darkness, the Doctor said,

"How tired are you, boys? Do you feel too worn out with tent-building and turtle-catching to give an hour or two to making your first acquaintance with tropical moths by night?"

There was little excuse for asking the question, as the Doctor well knew; for the young naturalists were not of the stuff that tires over such exertions, nor were they likely to confess to being tired when there was such an unusual proposition as the present made to them. Eagerly they began to gather together their nets and poison-bottles, while the Doctor took from his belongings a small bull's-eye lantern, and from their provision outfit a bottle of beer and one of molasses. Holding up the former, he said, laughingly,

"I hope you won't think that I am going to encourage the beer habit in you; on the other hand, I am going to give you an illustration of how it may, in certain cases, lead to downfall and death. If we were to go out to-night into the woods over there, depending on nothing but our eyes to detect an occasional passing moth, and with only our nets to capture them, I think we should deserve credit if we brought in one specimen apiece."

"I was just going to say that I didn't see how we were going to catch anything without a powerful lantern to attract them when I saw you unpack that bull's-eye.

What are you doing, Doctor? What in the world are you trying to make?" Harry added, as he noticed the Doctor mixing some of the beer in a tin cup with some molasses and adding some alcohol.

"I am making a much better magnet to attract the treasures we covet than my bull's-eye lantern, as you will presently see," was the reply.

After the Doctor finished mixing his "stomach-ache medicine," as Hal called it, and the boys had the rest of the outfit together, they started for the woods. This was a fringe of rather stunted logwood, iron-wood, cedar and other trees, growing in the hollows or valleys between the sand ridges formed by the action of the nearly constant sea-breeze. Here and there, where some extra high sand dune protected it from the wind, there was a tree larger than its fellows, and on the sides of these away from the wind, the Doctor stopped to put on a liberal coating of his mixture with a paint brush. This was slow work, for it had now grown quite dark, and the underbrush was so densely matted together, and there were so many places where creeping vines made stumbling likely, that the Doctor had to go ahead with the lantern and a cutlass to clear the way. After they had thus visited six or eight trees he said,

"Now let's go back to the first tree and see what there is there to interest us by this time. If I am not much mistaken in the night and the locality, we ought to find good proof that it is not always men who are lured by alcoholic stimulants to their ruin."

"You don't mean that that stomach-ache medicine is

likely to attract moths, do you? How would they know so soon that it was there? Will they feed on that mess?" queried Harry.

"The mess, as you call it," the Doctor answered, "not only attracts them and is a favorite food, once they scent it, but it is so attractive that it is pretty well known that they are able to scent it for long distances; perhaps a mile or more with a fair breeze, such as we have now. Here we are at our starting-point, and you can soon see what the mixture will do. However, it is just as well to tell you beforehand that if the wind is not quite right, or there are in the neighborhood any quantity of sweet-scented flowers, we may not have very good fortune."

The wind and other requirements evidently were favorable; for when they arrived in front of the tree, and the Doctor threw the light of the bull's-eye full on the beer-painted space, the boys were electrified to see gathered around it, or even in it, a host of beetles, bugs, and ants, with perhaps a dozen moths of various sizes, sipping the sweet mixture with their long tongues. The young hunters were for making a dash at this collection of coveted trophies, but the Doctor cautioned them with these words:—

"Take care, boys; they won't fly away. They are too fond of that drink and already feel the effect of the alcohol. All you need to do is to walk up to the tree, put your poison-bottle over the insect you want and then wait a moment until the fumes overpower it, when you can easily shake it into the bottle and put on the cork. Those fine big fellows, you will find, will allow you to lift them gently up by the bodies, so intent are they on more of this toddy, and they can be put in the chloroform box. The beetles and smaller fry can, one by one, be knocked into your alcohol bottles. You do not need to use your nets unless a new moth comes flying around while we are here."

Following the Doctor's advice, the boys soon had over a dozen fine moths, one of them nine inches across the wings, and a countless lot of other insects in their bottles, and it was with the greatest eagerness that they pushed forward to the next tree, anxious to see whether anything not at the first awaited them. But they were hardly prepared for the surprise that came.

"Look out! Look out! Hal," Ned shouted, as Harry stepped forward, with his poison-bottle open, just as the Doctor threw the light on the beer patch on the tree. "There! There, on the limb, just in the shadow; a monster snake!"

Hal, on whom his brother's frightened tones had already made sufficient impression to cause him to step back quickly, at the word "snake" jumped back some distance; while the Doctor, throwing the light where Ned directed, stepped forward cautiously, changing the lantern from his right to his left hand as he did so. Then making his last movements very stealthily, he slowly advanced on the snake, and, before the boys could imagine what he was going to do, in an instant the snake was dangling from his right hand which was tightly gripped around its slimy body just behind the swelled and gaping head. The boys were too startled to speak, at first, and before they could do so, the Doctor assured them of the absence of danger.

"This is a perfectly harmless snake, as are most of those found in these islands. It is closely related to the big "pine-snake" of our New Jersey and Pennsylvania woods, and, while it can squeeze pretty hard, is thoroughly non-poisonous for the very simple reason that it has no fangs or poison-teeth. If you will come closer here, and one of you hold the lantern while I hold its mouth open with a lead-pencil, you will see that its mouth is only provided with rows of small delicate teeth, with which it can hold a rat or toad, but there is no sign of fangs, which, were they there, would protrude from the upper row of teeth when its jaws are thus forced apart. As it is preparing to give my arm a good squeezing, I will let it go, now; but first I want you to notice its long, tapering tail. It is a very safe rule to follow that such tails denote in America a non-poisonous snake, while a blunt or abrupt end to a snake's tail nearly always means that it is of a dangerous kind."

"Why don't you kill it, anyhow, Doctor?" said Ned. "I can't say that I ever like snakes around, even if they are harmless."

"As a rule, it is always best to destroy as few of Nature's works as possible. What is known as the 'balance of Nature' is not to be trifled with; for these creatures all have their uses, and unless positively hurtful or injurious to man had better be left unmolested, save so far as the needs of museums and students require the death of a few of each sort. Then, too, we insect hunters ought always to consider snakes our allies. They feed on our worst enemies, the lizards and toads, who in a night devour more rare and valuable insects than all collectors will take in a generation."

So saying, he dropped the snake, which quickly disappeared in the bushes, and they all resumed their attentions to the second tree. Here, also, they found a store of living treasures waiting to be caught, and at each tree they found something new or surprising to interest them. So much was this so, that they could hardly believe it when the Doctor announced that it was after ten o'clock and high time that all respectable campers were in their tents.

CHAPTER V

COLUMBUS AND HIS LANDFALL

Foraging for Breakfast — Picking Oysters from Bushes — Wholesale Fishing — An Abandoned Garden — The Danger of Poisonous Pests — A Sumptuous Lunch — The Preservation of Insects — Flamingoes — Imaginative Historians — Columbus's Character — Which is the "Landfall"? — Indian Slavery — Columbus's Untruthfulness

NOTWITHSTANDING their late hours the night before, the boys were up soon after sunrise, and when the Doctor came from the tent, he found the fire already started and plenty of wood on hand for the breakfast cooking. He proposed, however, that instead of an early breakfast they walk along the beach and get a look at the early morning life and add a zest to their appetites.

"That suits me first rate," Hal replied; "but I feel already as though I could eat an elephant."

"All right, then, we'll have to catch two elephants for the lad," retorted Ned. "Let's see whether we can't find our breakfast in true explorers' style, just as we did last night, and not have to depend on those cans of stuff from New York that anybody can have."

The tide was going out, and the hard, firm beach made a delightful pavement. On this they found many specimens of two kinds of tiger-beetles new to them, several queer sea-shells, and some tiny crabs and jelly-fish. The former they collected, but with the latter two they contented themselves with mere examination, as the Doctor told them they could find plenty of the same things at the island of Great Inagua, where they would soon be, and from which point they could conveniently ship their trophies home. Further along they came across an inlet running back into the island, along the sides of which the mangrove bushes or trees grew down to the water's edge, and showed plainly that they stood deep in the water at high tide. Taking off his shoes and stockings, and rolling up his trousers, the Doctor waded into the shoal water and began to break off knotty lumps and pieces of the very rough bark, as they seemed to be, and put them in a basket he had brought along.

"What are you getting there, Doctor?" asked Harry, as the boys came up after a long chase after a particularly large dragon-fly which was out in search of an early morning meal.

"Oh, I'm getting some excellent eatables. You young men probably don't know that in this part of the world the oysters grow on trees."

"Oysters on trees! Really, Doctor, that is one too much! I know that they have *bread*-fruit, cocoanut *milk*, cacao *butter*, and I have heard, too, of vegetable *eggs* and of the *oyster*-plant of our own garden, but that real oysters are vegetables down here is beyond me, I confess," said Ned.

"No, not vegetables, but simply growing fast to these mangroves. The oyster is a high-water feeder who does not mind being high and dry at low tide, and hereabouts he attaches himself to these bushes in these clusters."

Tossing one of the big knotty masses on the beach as he spoke, the Doctor continued: "If you examine that lump, you will see that it consists of seven or eight very small oysters with their shells firmly grown together. They are tiny compared with some of our large kinds, but they are like our famed 'Blue Points' in flavor, and will make us a delightful lunch."

"What about breakfast? Where are those two elephants? my stomach is beginning to ask," said Harry.

"Well, what have you boys been catching all this time?" the Doctor asked, as he waded out and began looking over their captures. "Tiger-beetles, some half-grown grasshoppers, and a fine dragon-fly, eh! What kind of a breakfast do you think they would make? Not much, I guess. How would you like some nice yellow perch for breakfast?"

"That sounds something like it; but we ought to have them pretty soon now, judging from the way I feel," said Harry, while Ned laughingly added that Hal's symptoms were his also.

"Well, catch me a half-dozen young grasshoppers while I fix this line," the Doctor replied, as he took from his pocket a long fishing-line with a heavy lead sinker at the end, and, some distance above it, five short side-lines of horsehair with cork floats, and hooks at the end of each. Putting a grasshopper on each hook, he threw the sinker well into the middle of the inlet by first twirling it around his head and then releasing it so that the momentum would carry it far. This arrangement placed five kicking grasshoppers on the surface of the water about four feet apart, but almost as soon as the boys had observed this, there was a flash in the air near one of the corks, then another, and another, and the Doctor began hauling in the line. Much to the surprise of the boys, who were used to sitting by the half-hour "with nary a bite," as Ned said, there were four fine fish, ranging from eight to thirteen inches long, on the hooks, and the remaining hook was bare. This performance repeated twice added five more fish to their supply, making three good pan-fish to each one of them, and much elated they started home at a good pace. On the way back the Doctor explained to them that while he had called these yellow perches, he had only done so because they were most like that northern fish, and the boys would not know them by their Bahama name. The ease with which they were caught was due to the fact that in all probability that inlet had not been fished in a half-dozen times in the past ten years, so sparse was the population thereabouts.

While they were all busy washing up the breakfast dishes and talking over their recent experiences, Ned said:—

"On the way back to camp this morning I saw a place where there was a big lot of wild flowers, some very beautiful ones, growing together. I should think that ought to be a good place for butterfly collecting, this morning. What do you think, Doctor?"

"I noticed that place. I think it must be the site of some abandoned house, for some of the flowers there are not native; that is, they are wild now, but they have originally been brought from other lands. You have observed that

F

the natives are fond of flower gardens; I imagine that some one has had a cabin here. It does not take long in this tropical climate for a bamboo hut to fall to pieces, and vines and bushes to cover the ruins from sight, nor does it take long for introduced plants to become wild. Anyhow, it will be a good collecting field, I should say."

Soon they were at the collecting spot, which proved, by the presence of several upright posts densely covered with vines, to be an abandoned home, as the Doctor surmised. Petunias of several shades, lilies of various kinds, pinks, roses, and a number of plants quite new to the boys, were mixed in a wild profusion of vines and creepers that showed by their overbearing wildness that they, at least, were natives here. And over all this tangle of vegetable loveliness hovered and soared butterflies of a score of species. Here floated, lazily, great *Papilios*, their velvety black wings and golden bands making them seem the uniformed officers of the host. Everywhere darted lemon and honey-yellow butterflies of smaller sizes, acting as orderlies taking messages for their generals; while a host of blue and azure and red and brown ones were intent on gathering honey or playing at mad games of tag. This sight was too much for the boys, and with gasps of delight they each darted for the spot with uplifted nets.

"Hold on, boys, hold on!" cried the Doctor. "Before you rush in there so bravely, I want to utter a few words of warning. Odd as it may seem, the neighborhood of an abandoned house is always extra dangerous in the tropics. In the first place, the decaying wood of the house is most attractive to centipedes and scorpions, both of which are much more poisonous than any hornets with which you are acquainted. Tarantulas or trap-door spiders are always fond of garden spots, and a hot, open space in the surrounding growth, such as this is, is especially likely to attract coral snakes. Last night I told you there were but few poisonous snakes in the Bahamas, and so there are. However, an occasional coral snake of moderate size is found here just as it is in Florida; but we are not in danger of the rattlers that are so dangerous in that State.

"Either a scorpion or centipede would put you on the sick list for at least twenty-four hours, and a tarantula might, if a good-sized one, make it three days. But a coral snake would do even worse; and it might, although it is quite unlikely, end fatally, if a large female snake bit either of you. Coral snakes are bright red and easily seen; they are, also, sufficiently cowardly to get out of the way, if not surprised while asleep. Now be careful where you stoop down to pick up things from the ground, and come at once to me if stung even by a bee, as I am well prepared for emergencies."

Perhaps the boys seemed cautious at first, but the appearance soon wore off; for they were so surrounded by coveted treasures of the insect world, most of which were entirely new to them, that they forgot in a little while all about the Doctor's cautioning words. This had no bad result, however; for when noon arrived, and the Doctor told them of the hour, they came from their labors only the worse for the heat and muscular effort.

"Doctor, where were all those snakes and tarantulas,

hobgoblins and other bugaboos you told us about? I didn't see anything worse than some mighty big hornets; did you, Hal?" asked Ned.

Without a word, but beckoning the boys to follow, the Doctor walked to where the crumbling door-sill and step were still lying, and quickly turning the latter over exposed to view a half-dozen or more scorpions of various sizes and two or three big, hard-bodied "Thousand-leggars," or *millipeds*, curled up in the rotting wood-earth.

"Well! if that don't beat the Dutch!" exclaimed Harry. "Oh, Ned, look at that biggest scorpion! It's got about fifty little ones on its back."

"Yes," commented the Doctor, as he struck one after the other of the ugly creatures a blow with a stick, "that is the ordinary way adopted by the mother scorpion for protecting and carrying around her large family of baby scorpions." So saying, he deftly placed his butterfly net under her and lifted the whole colony, after which he quickly walked down to the water's edge and held the net under the surface until all were drowned.

"I thought you told us not to take life unnecessarily, Doctor."

"So I did; but this is a case of necessity, if we would go back there in safety. Scorpions are sure to abandon a retreat that has been uncovered, and these might have scattered around that garden. Besides that, what I said last night was not intended to apply to those creatures capable of doing man serious injury or harm."

For lunch they had oyster soup, a fish salad made from the remains of their breakfast, and some wild celery, gathered near by, and a famous dish of fried oysters, a meal that was hard to beat anywhere, as Ned said, and one that convinced them that the Doctor was as good a cook as he was a naturalist and a guide. Such a meal was bound to be hearty after their morning's work, and the Doctor told them that it would be much better to "take it easy" after lunch, and spend the heat of the early afternoon preparing and labelling their captures, and lolling around. Their tent was so constructed that they could soon untie the bottom strings and throw all four of the side flaps up on the roof, so as to turn it into an awning, under which the wind had full sweep, and where they could work or loll in comfort.

While butterfly hunting was their chief natural history pursuit, the boys had readily fallen in with a proposition, made by the Doctor, that they should collect in all departments of animal life, the specimens of which could be easily transported and easily sold to museums or collectors in the United States and Europe. In this way, as he explained, they would get a much more complete idea of nature, derive much more benefit and interest from their trip, and also be able to contribute a considerable amount towards their expenses. They could keep one set of all the specimens collected, thereby establishing a fine foundation for a private museum of their own, and the Doctor would attend to selling all the extra material for them. This plan pleased the boys greatly, and all insect life, all rare or beautiful birds, rare reptiles, lizards, fish, and all manner of sea life, it had been decided they should gather, while not forgetting to keep an eye open for any rare animals that might be around. Therefore, their morning's captures represented all seven of the orders of insects, three lizards, and a lot of spiders that the Doctor had caught.

Beetles and some bugs they put in alcohol vials, keeping them separate, and carefully labelling each vial with date and place of capture. Grasshoppers, some of the bugs, — such as tree-hoppers, plant-lice, and others likely to be spoiled in alcohol, — they packed carefully in little tin boxes full of dried sawdust, sealing them up with wax when full. Wasps, bees, flies, and very large bugs they mounted on pins especially made for that purpose, and pinned into tight tin boxes with cork-lined bottoms which, when full, were also sealed up. While butterflies, all moths over an inch across the wings, and dragon-flies they folded in triangular pieces of paper and packed away carefully in tin boxes, labelling each box with date and place of capture. The smallest moths they carefully did up in little cones of paper, and packed away in boxes filled loosely with sawdust or cork chips. All these boxes were of tin, so that white ants and other pests could not eat through them and destroy their contents, as they would quickly do if the boxes were of wood. As a further precaution against the entrance of pests while the boxes were yet unsealed, naphthalin or "tar-camphor" was kept in them in liberal quantities. Lizards and spiders were kept in alcohol jars.

After all this was finished it was after half-past three, and the Doctor said a half or three-quarters of an hour given to a nap on their hammock-bed would be a good investment of time. After this siesta they decided to take their guns and see what they could do towards providing something good for supper, and at the same time keep a lookout for any valuable birds that might be around. With this in view they struck off into the undergrowth along the dried bed of what was evidently a stream of some size during the heavy rains. Having followed it for some time, they came to a clearing in the centre of the undergrowth, filled with tall marsh grass and having unmistakable signs of connection with some arm of the sea, thus being a salt marsh. Just as they had stopped to consult as to which direction they had better take, Ned whispered:—

"Look at that bird. There's a flamingo!"

The Doctor motioned them to be quiet, and whispered that where there was one there were others, and that he would soon bring them nearer. Carefully taking a piece of paper from his pocket, he placed it between his flattened hands, much as boys do with a blade of grass when they want to whistle with it, and gently blew so as to make a noise not unlike the shrill piping of a young turkey. Immediately the bird in sight held its long neck straight up in the air, and began to look from side to side; in a moment more another head appeared above the waving grass, and then another and another, until there were six long flamingo necks waving back and forth in a most grotesque way. Fortunately the hunters were shielded from sight behind a tall clump of grass, where they could see, but not be seen. The Doctor whispered that to shoot them where they were would be only to kill them in an impenetrable marsh, from which they could not be brought, and that when he scared them up they would circle round over head once or twice and afford an excellent shot, for which the boys must be ready. So saying, he stopped his whistling and suddenly clapped his hands loudly. Instantly every flamingo took to wing, and in a moment after each bird appeared coming directly over them, about one hundred feet from the ground, and in single file.

"I'll take first; Ned, second; Hal, third," the Doctor had just time to say, when his gun rang out, followed quickly by those of the boys. Down came one flamingo, and only one. A fine specimen it was, in very full and brilliant pink plumage.

"Well, there are two pretty poor shots in this crowd. Who do you think they are, Doctor?" asked Ned.

"I really don't know that criticism is quite in place just at this rather embarrassing time," the Doctor replied, with a laugh, "but that was flamingo No. 1 that came down."

"How could you tell that? I thought I saw it was the bird that I shot at that fell," said Harry.

"I had two ways of telling. In the first place, I noticed that the leader was the only full-plumaged bird, which we now have, and then I knew beforehand that you boys couldn't kill a flamingo, if you did hit it. When did you last load your guns and with what?"

"I declare!" said Ned, with a shade of mortification in his face, "if we didn't have those shells with dust-shot in them that we put in to shoot humming-birds while at Nassau. That's a pretty simple performance on our part. But why didn't you tell us, Doctor, if you knew it all the time?"

THE DOCTOR'S GUN RANG OUT, FOLLOWED QUICKLY BY THOSE OF THE BOYS.

"For two reasons. In the first place, this has made an impression on your minds you are not likely soon to forget; and if I get into the habit of telling you how to look after such things, you will soon fall into the habit of depending on me, instead of on yourselves. In the second place, by the time we have skinned this flamingo, and also prepared its skeleton, which we must save, you will both be very glad there was only one, and not three of them, for it must all be done to-night."

After an hour or more of hunting in vain, they came to the conclusion that their day had contained quite enough of the eventful, and had been much better than they could expect the average to be in that respect. So they trudged contentedly home and to supper, which was less gamy, and much more commonplace, than had been the three previous meals.

While they were all busily engaged in cleaning up the breakfast dishes the next morning, a gun fired at sea attracted their attention, and they looked up to see their skipper, the trader, riding at anchor in the offing and the small-boat on its way ashore. This meant hurry and bustle, for they had not expected him before the afternoon; but in about an hour they were all packed up, all their trophies gathered together into their "Bank of England," as Harry called the big tin trunk in which their treasures were packed, and they were on board the "Belle of Nassau" bound for Cat Island, the nearest neighbor in the group.

With a spanking wind they found themselves in the afternoon skirting the east shore of Cat Island, for many years supposed to be the first landing-place of Columbus and his "Island of San Salvador." The Doctor told them to gaze closely at its long sandy stretch of uninteresting and unpicturesque shore, nowhere rising more than a comparatively few feet out of the water and singularly devoid of attractive vegetation. This he wanted them to photograph on their memories, as it would be interesting to them in their future studies in history. This, or one of its adjoining islands, it undoubtedly was that the discoverer first set foot upon, and the boys would do well to study their nature closely, he told them, so as afterwards to compare them with the glowing accounts given by historians of these spots.

"We had at school in one of our readers part of Washington Irving's description of the landing of Columbus, and that certainly made the island of San Salvador seem very attractive," said Ned.

"Yes," the Doctor replied, "Irving has been one of the principal sinners in this respect. He paints the island not as he knew it to be in fact, but as his imagination led him to fancy it. The discovery of the New World was, without doubt, the most important event in the history of the world since the time of Christ. But all historians, until those of the last few years, have made the mistake of giving to Columbus all the credit for that discovery. It is the fact, nevertheless, that had it not been made by Columbus in 1492, it would have been by Pedro Alvarez Cabral, who in 1500 lost his course on the way to the Cape of Good Hope in search of India, and found himself on the coast of Brazil. During these times, when every one is talking about the Columbian exposition at Chicago, it has been natural for writers and orators, really knowing but little of the subject, to make almost a god out of the discoverer."

"Columbus didn't start out to discover a New World, did he?" asked Harry.

"No; he had no other idea than to find the gold mines and spice groves of India; and he died without any idea that he was the discoverer we now know him to be. It was not until 1513, when Balboa, from the mountains near Panama, saw the Pacific Ocean, that it dawned upon the geographers of the time that it was a new continent that had been discovered."

"Was it not strange that an explorer and geographer like Columbus should not know that the countries he discovered were very different from India?" Ned asked.

"In the sense in which we use those terms Columbus was not an explorer or a geographer. The thirteen years of his life previous to his residence in Portugal had been spent as a pirate, and that sort of life was not likely to add much to his knowledge, or to anything but his extreme hunger for riches."

"A pirate! Oh, Doctor, do you really mean that?"

"Most certainly; although it was not as discreditable to him as it seems to us now, for then all seafaring people carried on piracy. As long as a century after his time we find 'good Queen Elizabeth' in partnership with her admirals, Drake, Hawkins, and Frobisher, in their piratical expeditions in these very seas, and dividing the plunder and cheating them in the division. It was probably his experience as a pirate which caused him to drive such a shrewd bargain with Ferdinand and Isabella of Spain, when at last they consented to send him on his first voyage."

"What was the bargain like, Doctor?" asked Ned, to whom history was a particularly interesting study.

"There were six important stipulations in the agreement. They were: first, that he should have for himself and heirs forever the title of Admiral of all lands and continents discovered; second, that he should be the Viceroy or Governor-General of those lands, and should have the right to nominate their governors; third, that he should have one-tenth of all pearls, precious stones, gold, and silver found in them; fourth, that he or his lieutenant should be the sole judge of all causes or disputes arising in them; fifth, that he should contribute one-eighth of the expenses, and share one-eighth of the profit of the expedition; and sixth, that all these rights should descend to his heirs forever. You see he had no small amount of his attention fixed on this world's goods."

"How is it, Doctor, that we know so little of his early life? At school we were told to write a composition about him, and there were some of us who called him an Italian, some a Spaniard, and one or two thought he was from Portugal," Ned said.

"It is generally believed that the difficulty of gaining information at this late day is due to the fact that his principal biographer, his son Ferdinand, after he became a courtier and grandee of Spain, carefully suppressed and destroyed all proofs of his father's humble origin and life."

While this conversation was taking place, Harry, while listening, had been looking over the chart of the Bahamas which the Doctor had brought with them, and now suddenly looked up and said,

"This map has three islands marked in this way: Cat Island, supposed San Salvador; Watling's Island, landfall of Columbus; Atwood Key or Samana, supposed San Salvador. Now which of these is right, anyhow? They can't all be right!"

"That is a question which has been in dispute for three hundred years, and which now is not likely ever to be settled. There are so many doubtful points on which it depends that unless other manuscripts are discovered, — a most unlikely thing to happen, — we shall probably always be in doubt about it."

"Why, I should think it would be very easy to take Columbus's log-book, which I remember that he kept, and prove by that where he first landed; or why could they not find out which islands the natives knew by the name that he says was theirs for his landfall. I forget the name; what was it, Doctor?" asked Ned.

"Guanahani," the Doctor replied, and then continued: "In the first case, it is hard to follow Columbus's log-book for three reasons: first, because he was not sufficiently skilful in the use of Spanish to express himself accurately; second, because he kept a false account of his distances to deceive his dissatisfied sailors; and third, because we are in something of doubt as to just what he understood by a mile. Then again, we are not quite sure just where he first made a harbor in Cuba, so that we cannot follow him back from that point through all these islands to the point of his first land. As to your idea that the native memories of early names could help you, it is only necessary to say that in twelve years from the time Columbus landed here there was not one native left above the ground, although he had found the islands more populous than they now are."

"Gracious, how did that come about?" asked Harry.

"It was entirely due to the policy that the Spaniards established in dealing with these poor, ignorant, but peaceable wretches. Columbus speaks of their intelligence, of their kindly disposition, and his son writes of him as 'a dove bearing the olive branch of peace and the oil of baptism to the heathen'; yet, on their first Sabbath on land we find them kidnapping the unsuspecting natives and bearing them away to slavery. The first bishop sent out to the West Indies soon returned in disgust, saying that he could not endure seeing the cruelties practised on the natives. Under the pretence of converting them, they enslaved and sold these poor wretches into Spain for some time after the sovereigns had forbidden the practice. So you see it has been many long years, — over three hundred and fifty in fact, — since there were any natives left to help us in settling this question."

"Doesn't Columbus somewhere describe his landfall so that it can be told from the other islands?" asked Ned.

"There again we are interfered with in our search for the true San Salvador. For example, he tells us that his landfall was watered by many streams and produced many fruits; now, as a fact, there is no island in the whole

Bahamas well watered, and there is the best of reasons for feeling sure that there never was; and as to fruit, what there is here, now, is almost all of introduced varieties, brought by the English from other tropical countries. Every island he visited during that first voyage, he describes as better than the last; and as the first is described as something rather better than an earthly paradise, this at last becomes laughable. Of the trees on these islands, he wrote that there were 'many of them which had branches of many kinds, although growing from one trunk; and one branch is of one kind and another of another kind, and so different, that the diversity of the kinds is the greatest wonder of the world; for instance, one branch had leaves like those of cane, and another like those of mastic; and thus on a single tree were five or six of these kinds.' Of course there were no such trees in existence then, as there are none now, but the story was a very good one to awaken interest at home with."

"The only helpful things that he says of his San Salvador," the Doctor continued, "are that it bore green trees, was flat, surrounded by reefs, had a lagoon in it, and was an east and west island. These were, none of them, peculiarities of any one island, but belonged to several. Cat Island, however, has no lagoon, runs north and south, and it has the highest land in the Bahamas on it, so that it is least likely of all to be spoken of as a flat island. Watling's Island, on the other hand, has nearly one-third of its interior taken up by a lagoon and it is decidedly flat; but it, too, runs north and south."

"Then you think that Watling's Island is the true landfall, don't you, Doctor?"

"No; I can hardly say that," was the reply. "Cat Island is favored by Irving the historian and Von Humboldt the explorer and naturalist; but neither of them was aware of all that is now known on the subject, and they were not practical sailors. Turk's Island was considered to be the landfall by Navarette the historian; but his theories have been thoroughly exploded, as have also those of Varnhagen, who claimed Mariguana for that distinction. Watling's Island, which, according to Munoz the historian, Captain Becher the geographer, Lieutenant Murdock of our navy, and many navigation authorities of our country and Great Britain, is the true landfall, is certainly better entitled to the honor than any of those I have just mentioned. But in a few days we will visit Atwood Key, or Samana, which, in common with some of the most careful geographers and navigators, among them Captain Fox, Dr. Redway, and Fiske the historian, I believe to have the most evidence in its favor as the original Guanahani, or San Salvador. It, better than any other, answers all the descriptions of Columbus; it is flat, is an 'east and west island,' has a lagoon, and from it his course can best be followed to the point he is supposed to have first reached on the coast of Cuba."

After supper that night, as they were all sitting at the bow watching the little vessel plough its way through the phosphorescent sea, throwing up, with each wave, a glistening shower of diamonds and amethysts, rubies and emeralds, Ned suddenly asked:—

"Doctor, is it certain that there may not have been great changes in these islands in four hundred years, and that we may be doing Columbus injustice in thinking him so careless in his description?"

"Of course there may have been some changes in the elevation and general appearance of these islands, due to earthquakes and the ocean's action. Cuba, Haiti, and Jamaica are all known to have subsided perceptibly within two hundred years. But that would not account for most of his errors, I regret to say. I wish it would, my boy, for I do not like to fill the rôle of iconoclast."

"Ike who? I don't think I ever heard of the gentleman before," said Harry, whose reverence for big words was not very great, as yet.

"Iconoclast, a breaker of images; one who shatters idols and pulls down and overthrows our accepted theories. I would much rather think of Columbus as Irving and others profess to believe him to have been, than otherwise, but there are too many things well known about him to allow me to do so. To excuse my attitude in the matter, let me tell you this one thing about his second voyage. When he was about to return to Spain, and being anxious to prove to the King that he had discovered the other side of India, he called together eighty of his men and compelled them, under heavy penalties, to take oath before his notary that it was possible to go from Cuba to Spain by dry land through and across Asia. These men he threatened with having their tongues wrenched out should they depart from this oath on their return; yet he must have known it to be false swearing, for he was acquainted with the island nature of Cuba. Bernaldez, a priest with whom he lived, tells us that, while a man of but little learning, 'he was of an ingenious turn of mind'; and he certainly showed it then."

It was by this time quite late; but the boys said, as they started off to bed, that they could listen to these bits of history all night, especially while they were sailing through the very waters under discussion.

CHAPTER VI

THE DEVIL-FISH

In Camp again — Negro Honesty — The Geographical Sense — Marvellous Memories — Training the Memory — The Collector's Outfit — Comparative Abundance of Butterflies — Spanish Cedar — A Devil-fish at Home — A Three-hearted Monster — The Dreaded "Kraken"

WHEN they came on deck the next morning, they found the vessel riding idly at anchor, with some of the crew washing down the deck, while others were rowing the trader-skipper ashore in the small-boat. They were in a small half-moon-shaped harbor protected by coral reefs, and about a quarter of a mile from the shore; and it took but one comprehensive look around to impel Ned to say:—

"All these Bahama harbors seem to be the same, over and over; only the village or town near by changes somewhat, and even that but little. I don't wonder it is impossible to tell where Columbus first landed; I don't see how any one could describe these different harbors so that the next comer could tell one from another. Where are we now, Doctor?" he asked.

"We are in the harbor which many geographers agree is where Columbus first landed and took possession of American soil. This is Watling's Island, which I told you so much about last night, and this harbor is perhaps as likely to be the point of Columbus's landing here as any.

The adherents of this island as the landfall have no more decided differences with their opponents than they have among themselves as to which of the bays he entered here.

"As the captain has a brother living here," he continued, "who is a part owner in the trading business, he expects to remain for at least two days; so I told him that when the boat which is now taking him ashore comes back, we will pack our necessary articles into it and have the men row us around that point of land, where we can camp, free from the prying eyes of natives, until he is ready to sail away. How does that suit?"

"That's fine," Harry rejoined. "Camping out beats hotels and steamers, and much more so this little tub."

By the time the boat came back the party had made a hearty breakfast and had their belongings ready to load. Much to the delight of the boys, there was a strong, well-shaped, two-oared rowboat in tow behind the other, which the Doctor told them they were to have the use of during their stay, as they would be encamped on the shore of an inlet which ran for some distance into the island, and a boat would enable them to hunt and fish with greater comfort.

It was about half-past nine when they and their outfit were all safely on shore, and the Doctor proposed that they simply pack their things away in the shade of some cedar trees, while they started off at once on a butterfly hunt, for time was valuable. They would have plenty of time to unpack things after lunch, and the hours from ten to one were always best for insect-collecting. With this they readily agreed, Harry only asking:—

"Is it safe to leave all our things this way, without hiding them? It isn't so far around the point to the village but that some one could easily walk over here and help himself."

"Don't let that worry you, Hal," the Doctor replied. "Wherever you go in the English West Indies you can feel pretty safe in such matters. The black people will sometimes help themselves to food that is around lose, or to some trinket or little things of no real value; but they have too slight need for most of the things we consider valuable, and the Queen's laws are too well and promptly enforced, for us to worry over such dangers. In the French and Spanish West Indies it is a different thing; but here we are quite safe."

"Now, I propose that we row up the inlet about a mile to where an elevation in the shore marks the place of an old Lucaya Indian shell-heap, and from which we can survey our way to the best collecting spot," the Doctor continued.

"How do you know there is such a mound there, Doctor? it isn't mentioned on our maps," asked Ned.

"I was here and camped on that mound for five days nine years ago next month," was the reply; "and I remember this region, as though it was yesterday that I last saw it."

"Do you always carry all the places you have visited in your mind, that way?"

"Yes, I think I do. My sense of location is very largely developed; the 'geographical sense,' it is called. And my memory is in very good order."

"I should say it is!" Harry commented. "Ned and I were talking about that the other day, and we couldn't see how you could remember so many facts, figures, dates, and the names of persons and places. But the most wonderful part to us is how you can remember all the terrible, jaw-breaking scientific names that you know for every plant and animal we bring you or talk about. We agreed we would ask you how you do it, and how many such names you think you remember."

"It has been estimated that Victor Hugo remembered and accurately used over 8000 words in his ordinary work as a writer; Cuvier, the French naturalist, and Louis Agassiz, the Swiss zoölogist, could promptly give the names, according to careful estimates, of over 5000 animals, in addition to the ordinary words they knew perfectly. It has been said of Dr. Asa Gray, the great botanist of Harvard, that he knew quite 8000 plants by name and at sight. But by far the most remarkably-trained memory with which I have had acquaintance was that of Dr. Joseph Leidy, for many years and until his death President of the Academy of Natural Sciences of Philadelphia, the collections of which, you remember, we stopped to inspect on our way from your home to New York. Dr. Leidy was not only a foremost geologist and mammalogist, having hundreds upon hundreds of the terms of these sciences upon his tongue's end; but he was a very good student of birds, reptiles, fishes, insects, and lesser things, and remarkably ready in remembering where their different species belonged in the great order of nature. Besides this he was an authority on microscopic life, especially minute parasites, was a fair botanist, one of the leading physicians and anatomists of his time, and a perfect encyclopædia of geography and exploration. Add to all this a good memory for names and faces, and a familiarity with several foreign languages, and you get some idea of this man's powers in that respect. After a long conversation with him one day, on this subject, I estimated that his memory enabled him to use 25,000 words at will, and I estimated it thus: —

" Ordinary English words		3000
" French "		2000
" German "		2000
" Latin "		2000
English technical "		5000
Medical and anatomical words		5000
Geological and zoölogical names		3000
All other scientific		3000
Geographical and personal		2000
		25,000

"This seems almost beyond belief, I know; but that it is a very safe and moderate estimate I am sure. It is far greater than most men do possess, because few men are masters of so many and different subjects as he was. And it is far greater than most men can possess, because few are born with the talent for memorizing, and still fewer have the patience to train what they have got. For a memory can be trained just as well as a muscle can."

"How have you trained your memory, Doctor? Yours is far ahead of anything I thought possible," asked Ned.

"To educate the memory, one must learn first how not to abuse it. The athlete who wants to get his muscles in perfect condition learns first what an overtax on them is, and never does that. To have the memory a storehouse of useful facts, it is necessary to place no useless work upon it. Never read 'trashy' books, pass by all sensational matters, such as murders, suicides, accidents, and the like, in newspapers; read only such matter as you feel you will be proud to know hereafter. Never tire the memory; if any sort of brain work seems tiresome or unusually hard to do, stop it at once, if you can, and take up some pleasanter occupation. As far as possible do the work that is to remain in the brain between nine and twelve in the morning, and eight and eleven at night. Where it is possible to associate the word to be memorized with some form, do so. It is much easier, and far more useful, to associate the name *Felis leo* with the lion's form than not to do so; and it is much easier to remember the volcano of Cotopaxi, if its place on the map of Ecuador and a picture of it are associated with the mere word."

By this time they had reached the shell mound, and climbing ashore, the Doctor fastened the boat, while the boys unloaded their collecting material. The collecting outfit carried by each was quite simple, when the many different ways in which their captures had afterwards to be prepared were considered. Their coats were provided with four deep outside pockets, in two of which they carried an alcohol bottle with a wide mouth and a glass stopper, and another of the same form in which the deadly *potassium cyanide* was mixed with plaster of Paris in the bottom, thus being laden with a dangerous vapor which almost instantly killed such insects as were not to be placed in alcohol. The other two pockets were reserved for the triangular, ready-folded papers into which their butterflies were placed, one pocket holding the empty papers, the other those that were filled. By a strap, a tin box, somewhat larger than a cigar box, and lined with cork, hung from the shoulder, into which were placed those insects that required to be pinned in the field; and last, though by no means least, they were armed with a stoutly made net, consisting of a polished hickory handle with a strong brass ring about fifteen inches in diameter firmly fastened to it, and a bag-shaped net, of medium heavy bobbinet, a yard deep. This was their insect-hunting outfit complete, save that each had a pair of steel forceps to use in picking up such insects as had "very warm ends," as Harry said of the wasp and bee tribe.

Inside, their coats were provided with large game-pockets, extending all the way around, into which other trophies could be put; and to enable them to fill these, each carried, fastened to a belt and over his right hip, a very long-barrelled pistol of 32 calibre, to which a skeleton shoulder-piece could quickly be attached, so as to turn it into a very fair shot-gun for light use. A few cartridges loaded with shot, and a dirk-knife in a leather sheath on the belt at the left side, intended for use in cutting their way through bushes and like work, completed the outfit; which, although it sounds quite formidable, did not weigh, all told, over eight pounds, or less than a good, full-sized gun.

"Doctor," said Ned, after they had been collecting for some time along the edge of a swamp in which there were flowers attractive to insects, "do you know that I am a little disappointed in the number of insects, and especially of butterflies, that we see. I thought we'd find the air here in the tropics alive with them, hundreds of kinds and thousands of specimens. But I don't know that there are really as many in one place as I have seen on a hot day in Pennsylvania. How is it? Is this a poor time of the year?"

"No," was the reply; "on the contrary, it is the best time, in my opinion. But there is one thing you forget, and that is, that these creatures keep appearing here every month in the year, and do not have to come forth in hosts during a comparatively few weeks of very warm weather, as they do in the north. The greatest crowds and flocks of butterflies are to be seen far in the north, even up in Labrador and Lower Alaska; but there one will find very few kinds, but very many individuals of each kind, and all within about six weeks. Under the equator the number of kinds are legion, but they do not flock forth in clouds in a short time. At Ega, on the Amazon River, for example, there have been more kinds of butterflies taken in a radius of five miles from the town than are known to exist in the entire United States.

"Then, too," he continued, "insects have much more to feed upon here, and consequently their flight is much less general, as a rule, than it is in a country where so much of the land is under cultivation, that all for a long distance round come to some rich swamp or honey-laden clover field. Collecting in the tropics is a work requiring more ceaseless care, more going in search of good localities, and much endurance of heat. Nor is it possible to chase butterflies here as in the north, for here everything is too densely overgrown with vegetation for that."

After lunch, and an hour of idleness in the shade of some cedar trees, they put up the tent near the edge of the inlet, where the Doctor thought they would get the best breezes during the hot hours. While they were at this work, Harry asked:—

"Doctor, why do they call these trees cedars? They certainly are not like those we know by that name."

"The Spanish cedar, known to botanists as *Cedrela odorata*, is not in any sense a cedar, but is one of the mahogany family, as its appearance, and the grain of its wood, which you have often seen in cigar-boxes, shows. Its name cedar probably comes to it from the odor of the wood, which is not unlike that of our cedar."

Later in the afternoon it was proposed that they row along the shores of the inlet, as it was low tide, and gather some oysters for supper, together with such other treasures as they could find. While they were engaged at this work, along a part of the shore where there was a considerable mass of coral rock much hollowed out by the action of the water, Ned suddenly exclaimed:—

"What in the world is that, Doctor? Look, there in the water! A great bunch of giant eels!"

Looking down into the crystal water, they could all plainly see a lot of thick, squirming, snake-like bodies, slowly moving up and down with a gentle motion, and all, apparently, with one end running into a hole in the rock.

Ned was for trying some bait on a strong line in the endeavor to catch one or more of them; but Harry favored reaching boldly down and grabbing one with the hands. While they thus planned, the Doctor listened with interest, until Hal started to put his plan into execution, when he quickly said: —

"Hold on there, Hal! That won't do! Those eels, as you call them, all belong to one creature, and it is an *octopus*, or devil-fish, that you are looking at. He is probably much better able to pull you down than you are to bring him up here."

"A devil-fish!" exclaimed Ned. "Well, I rather guess we don't want to fool with him. Why, if half I've read about them is true, I guess we'd better be rowing home."

"Probably not nearly half of it is true," the Doctor said, laughing, as he unwound a ball of strong grass cord from his pocket; "for there is nothing, probably, on the earth or in the sea, about which more 'fish stories' have been told. But I guess we can fix him so that when we leave here he will come along with us."

While saying this he had tied a running noose in the end of the cord, and, then, with a smaller cord, he tied a piece of raw meat, brought along for bait, so that it hung loose in the loop of the noose.

"Now, you boys take the oars and quietly put the stern of the boat in right over where Mr. Devil-fish is, and when I give the word, you both pull for dear life until I say stop, and pull right for deep water in the centre of the inlet."

Then bending over the stern, he gently let the noose down; in an instant he gave a quick jerk, and immediately began to haul in the cord, while he called to them to pull away rapidly. In a few moments they were in mid-stream, and, after making the cord fast, he turned and explained that he had the beak of the devil-fish fast in the noose and was towing it behind, with enough rope out to prevent its getting hold of the boat, and not enough to allow it to reach the bottom and hold fast. The beak, he explained, was the only part that it would not tear out to liberate itself.

"I read once of an English navy officer," Ned began, "who was stopping at a hotel in the tropics, and who came down to dinner in full evening uniform, white trousers and all. Finding he had a half-hour to spare, he strolled along the beach, looking for shells. He came suddenly upon an *octopus*, I think it was, or a cuttlefish, that was sheltered in a hollow in a rock. He stood and eyed it, and in return it looked steadily at him, and for quite a little while they were both motionless, just glaring at each other. Suddenly, without any warning, the *octopus* threw at him a stream of inky stuff that drenched his beautiful white trousers, and left him wishing he had not tried to stare a devil-fish out of countenance while he was in his best togs."

"Could that yarn be true, Doctor?" Harry asked. "Do they throw ink around that way; and are they easily made mad?"

"There is nothing improbable in the story, as we shall doubtless see, when we come to get this prize ashore."

When they approached the shore and go into shoal water, the Doctor drew their captive still closer to the boat to keep him from getting hold on the bottom, where he would fasten himself and drag some of his arms loose. Then he directed Ned to wade ashore and get one of their carving-knives, and tie the handle of it firmly to one of the butterfly-net handles. With this makeshift spear he reached over the stern, and drawing the creature up until it was almost on the surface of the water, he struck it three or four blows in the body, so as to place it beyond the chance of giving active battle, although it still showed signs of life, and made a feeble resistance against coming ashore. While this was going on the water was clouded; first light, then dark brown, and finally nearly black; while the creature itself changed from pink to red, to blue and to purple.

After its struggles had been brought to a close by a well-directed stab, they gathered around it, while the Doctor explained its structure and told something of its nature.

"This is a true *octopus*, or 'eight-legger,' as the name might be translated, and, therefore, it belongs to the family of *Cephalapodæ*, a word derived from the two Greek words meaning head and feet, used because, as you see, its feet, or tentacles, grow out of the forward part of its head. It has a soft, fleshy, roundish, egg-shaped body, which ends in fleshy fins. The head protrudes sufficiently to be distinct from the body, and has a well-formed mouth, or beak, a large pair of eyes, and a good hearing-apparatus. The eyes are capable of being protruded on short, fleshy stalks, and its gaze is decided, and even threatening, and their fiery, golden-colored centres have a sort of fascination about them. The mouth," he continued, turning the creature over, "is here, in front of the head, and is armed with a cruel pair of horny or shell-like jaws, giving it a beak strongly resembling that of a parrot. Its legs terminate in suckers, which it uses to attach itself to objects, to hold its prey, or in moving about; and they are frequently armed with sharp, horny claws."

"It feels almost like jelly," Ned said, as he pressed one of its legs with his foot."

"Yes, so it does, and so free from skeleton is it that, save its beak and the central body and head, it can lose any part of its fleshy mass and reproduce it again at will," the Doctor replied. Then he continued: "It has three hearts — one about the centre of its body, and one near each of the gills, on the head; it can lose either of the latter, but a cut that reaches the former, as did my last blow, soon despatches it."

"I noticed it change color very beautifully, just as we were hauling it out," said Harry.

"Yes, instead of being content to blush red or turn white with anger, as do we, it can change its complexion to quite a score of different colors and shades; but that is not all, for it will cover itself, if very angry or very much frightened, with pustules, warts, and long hair-like threads, so wonderful is its muscular control of its outer covering. For many centuries the inky fluid it emits was used for writing-purposes, and to-day the extract made from the color sac is much used in water colors under the name of sepia. So strong and indestructible is it, that the black material taken from the sacs of fossil species, dead and turned to stone thousands of years ago, readily makes a brilliant sepia."

The specimen that they had captured measured two feet and seven inches across its extended legs, which the Doctor told them was a good-sized one for that region. Yet its body was quite small, giving it much the appearance of a gigantic water-spider; a most repulsive and hideous monster. The Doctor said that, as they had no jar large enough to hold it, and it would take more than all their alcohol to preserve it, it was best to throw it away as soon as Ned finished a pencil sketch of it, which he had by this time started.

After their supper of broiled and fried oysters, and some guava preserves and bananas that they had brought ashore, while they were cleaning up the cooking-things, Harry, whose mind still ran on their recent capture, said:—

"Don't devil-fishes grow to be very large and savage, Doctor? And do they lay eggs in quantities, like fish?"

"They lay from twenty to thirty pear-shaped eggs in a cluster, that looks like a bunch of black grapes, and is securely fastened to some stationary object under water. The sailors call these 'sea-raisins,' and the mother devil-fish stays by them, and is very savage during the month they are hatching. There are modern stories of their having grown to be thirty feet across, but about ten feet appears to be the greatest size known beyond doubt. In ancient days they were known as 'kraken,' and were credited with power to drag a three-masted ship beneath the waves; and one old naturalist, and a bishop at that, tells of one on the back of which a thousand soldiers could have been drilled. These stories were so generally believed that even Linnæus, the great naturalist, proposed the name of *Sepia macrocosmos*, 'the great sepia,' for the giant kind. However, they grow quite large enough to be formidable enemies; for although slow and clumsy on land, their movements are lightning-like in the water, and a man would there have no chance for his life in the clutches of one."

"Has any one ever been attacked by a large one?" Harry asked.

"It is time we started to try our molasses-and-beer trick on the moths; but as we go along, I will tell you of one well-known case," the Doctor said.

"A Mr. Beale, a naturalist," the Doctor began, "was walking on the shore of a tropical island, when he saw an extraordinary-looking animal crawling back towards the surf on eight soft, bending legs. As it appeared to be alarmed and was doing its best to escape, he tried to stop it by stepping on its legs, but it easily liberated itself. Then he grabbed one of its legs, held firmly, until it looked as if it would pull apart, and then gave it a powerful jerk. This so enraged it, that with a spring it left the ground, and, winding its cold, slimy legs around his bare arm, attempted to fasten its beak, which he then first noticed, in his flesh. He cried loudly for help, and he was released by a companion, only by cutting it away from him bit by bit. It was over four feet across, although its body was little bigger than a large orange. He described the effects of its clammy grasp, horrible form, and glistening eyes as sickening and terrible beyond words. But here we are at a good tree for 'sugaring.'"

Their success was about as on the former night, and they returned late, laden with treasures, and thoroughly tired by another eventful day.

CHAPTER VII

DOWN THE ISLANDS

Migrating Butterflies — Samana or Guanahani — A Tropical Downpour — Meeting Old Friends — An Island "Pooh-Bah" — Camping on Great Inagua — Pugnacious Ants — Insect Pests — Their Sense of Smell — The Use of the Antennæ

THE following day was an uneventful one, the boys adding to their collections larger series of species already discovered, that they might have ample material from which to fill all orders. On the morning of the day after, the "boom" of a gun in the harbor warned them that their skipper was preparing to leave and that they must hurry with their packing to join him. Soon the small-boat appeared in the inlet, for the light row-boat that they had been using was hardly large enough to carry them and all their belongings through the higher waves of the harbor in safety; and in a little while thereafter they had bidden good-bye to Watling's Island, and were bounding along under full sail on their way to Atwood Key or Samana.

That afternoon, as he was lolling in a hammock on the after-deck, Harry suddenly exclaimed: —

"Hello! look up there! I declare if there aren't a lot of butterflies flying overhead, way out here at sea!"

As far as the eye could reach there extended a scattered column of butterflies flying rapidly along towards the southeast, and as far as they could see back of them others could be seen coming towards them. This was a most unaccountable sight to the boys, and the wonder of it was deepened when the Doctor pointed out another column, further to the north and flying parallel to this, and told them that, no doubt, there were others out of sight.

"There must be several hundred in sight here, right near us," Ned exclaimed. "Then how many must there be in all of these two columns?"

"Go to the man at the wheel and ask him if he has noticed them, and whether he ever saw such a thing before," the Doctor suggested.

In a moment Ned returned with a look of bewilderment on his face, as he said: —

"What do you suppose? He says they were flying this morning about sunrise, and that they were passing over Watling's Island all day yesterday. And he says it isn't an uncommon sight at all at this time of year, and they always fly in about that direction. Where do you suppose they are going, Doctor? I hadn't any idea that butterflies flew in flocks this way, just like birds."

"The migrating habit is well known in some butterflies," the Doctor replied, "and it is not alone in the tropics that it is observed. I remember seeing a migration of the large red *Danais archippus*, so common in our North, along the banks of the upper Delaware River in New Jersey, which was headed due south, and kept up in the face of a head wind pretty steadily all of two days. In the Tennessee mountains I also once saw a migration

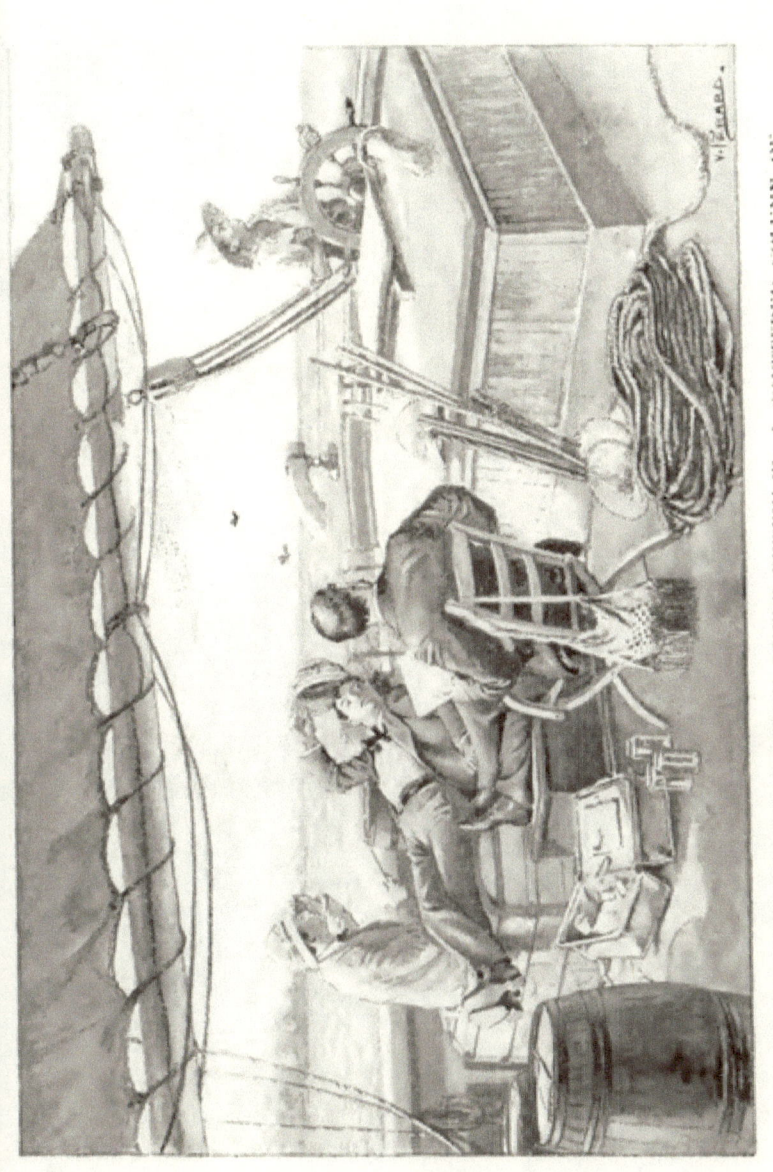

AS FAR AS THE EYE COULD REACH THERE ENTENDED A SCATTERED COLUMN OF BUTTERFLIES.

of a similar species also bound towards the warm lowlands of the far South. In Jamaica I have seen a species, common in Florida and Georgia, but rare in Cuba and Jamaica, passing overhead bound south for three days, and learned from a ship, just in from Cartagena, Colombia, that they had been passing them for two days. In all of these cases they were facing a warm wind, and in every case of which I have full information that seems to be their custom. So I am of the opinion that it is either for a change of climate or to escape the coming heavy rains that they migrate, and that it is by the wind, in some way, that they decide where to go. From Florida to Jamaica is nearly five hundred miles, and on to South America nearly five hundred miles more. No doubt thousands perish in the sea, but I believe that thousands reach their destination in safety."

"Do they come back the next season?" Harry asked.

"No; that is the strange part of it. No one has ever observed any return migration, so far as I can ascertain. In all cases these columns are composed almost entirely of males, and they are usually of a species in which the few females that do live through the winter to deposit their eggs in the spring manage to find shelter from the cold in hollow logs, under stones, and in other safe places. Butterflies do not live so long that the same ones could come back next season, as a rule, and this migrating appears to be without reason, and of no benefit to the species.

"Mr. Belt, a collector in Nicaragua," the Doctor continued, "tells of a migration of a common species of that region, in which there were hundreds in sight at once, and which continued for weeks, so that it must have consisted of millions of individuals. Mr. Bates saw the same on the Amazon River several times, but in his case many of them settled on the margin of the river, and as they were a bright lemon-yellow species, much like these passing now, they made the shore look as though it was variegated with beds of crocuses and jonquils. And many other naturalists have observed this in various parts of the world; so you see migrating among butterflies is no new thing."

"Then you know the kind of butterfly those up there are, do you, Doctor?" asked Ned.

"Yes; both by the motion of their flight and the outline of the wings, seen through these field glasses, I can tell the genus they belong to, and I know that it can be but one species that in this locality is so very plentiful. It is *Callidryas cubule*, the largest sulphur-yellow butterfly without any black on its wings, that you have been catching so many of, the past few days."

"Is there no way to attract some of them down here to us?" asked Ned.

"Not on a moving vessel, I think; but if they were flying overhead on land, we might be able to attract them by a cloth of yellow color spread on the shore. That they would be likely to mistake for a gathering of their own kind, and some would come down to join them."

They reached Atwood Key about midnight, but it was not until the next morning that the boys got a glimpse of the land which the Doctor's arguments made them regard as the original landfall of San Salvador, the Guanahani of the early Lucaya Indians. With the exception of Mariguana it was, he told them, the only "east and west" island of all those fixed upon by various students of the subject; and Mariguana had none of the other requirements for filling Columbus's meagre description, and this one had every one of them to a nicety and had, besides that, the sanction of the old map made in 1500 by Juan de la Cosa, and another of about 1532 made by order of Henry II. of France, in both of which the names Guanahani and Samana are given to the same island.

Naturally, although the skipper intended to land here but for a few hours, the boys wanted to go ashore, even if only for a few minutes, so as to say that they had set foot on such historic ground. Therefore, with only their collecting outfits they went ashore in the boat with the skipper, agreeing not to wander far away and to be at the landing point soon after the gun was fired. But they had calculated on a continuation of the charmingly even clear weather of the past two weeks, without any regard for the few scattered, fleecy clouds away on the horizon. They had not been on shore over a half-hour, however, before great drops, seemingly out of a clear sky, began to fall. The Doctor, looking up and seeing the margin of the cloud just over them and that the set of the wind was in their direction, quickly directed them to undress completely. Astonished beyond measure, but observing that he was setting the example, they did as told. Then he told them to roll shirts and stockings inside of trousers, and those in their coats, tying the whole into the tightest possible bundle and putting it in the large pith helmet, that each wore to ward off the sun and keep his head cool. All this he showed them how to do, then tied the shoes of each closely under his bundle and the whole outfit in a protecting tree, hat side up, too far above the ground to be splashed by the downpour, that by this time was upon them.

"Now a tropical rain shower means the opening of the clouds and pouring the water out, as you will soon see; what would be called a 'water spout' or 'cloud burst' in your State is a daily occurrence during the rainy season here. At this time of year a shower will last only a few moments, but so great is its force that we should soon be drenched through. The temperature will go down perceptibly during it, and there is the danger. If we got wringing wet and well chilled in this shower and had to wait until we reached the vessel again to get dry clothes, even such an old stager as I might get a touch of fever, but you boys would need extra doses of quinine for three or four weeks to come, and might be quite sick. Now that we may not get chilled we will place our collecting-bottles, nets, and guns here, and take a gentle run around them until the sun comes out again."

So they did; and when, in about twelve or fifteen minutes, the cloud had passed over, they had dry clothes to put on again and were none the worse for the wetting, after their return to the vessel, save that their guns and collecting-boxes needed a good drying out and cleaning.

As they left the harbor that afternoon, the skipper told the Doctor that he had disposed of all his goods, and, beyond a short stop at Fortune Island, where he had to leave a package, he did not need to stop again until Great

Inagua was reached, at which point he expected to find goods awaiting him from the last New York vessel, which he would sell on his way back to Nassau, passing through the more westward islands. This exactly suited the Doctor, as there was now nothing in particular to keep them longer in the Bahamas, except the packing and shipping of some of their treasures to be sent home from Great Inagua.

On the morning of the next day as they rode at anchor in the harbor of Fortune Island, they were surprised to hear a hoarse steam whistle not far away, and, on looking up from the work of preparing some of their specimens for shipping, to see a fair-sized ocean steamship bearing in their direction. After a moment's scrutiny the Doctor said,

"That's an Atlas Liner; I can tell by its pearl-gray hull and the colors on its smokestack. It is stopping here, as they do every trip, either to take up blacks to help load and unload or to put them down again. The negroes in Haiti and Jamaica are so independent that it pays best to get such labor, as they will need in those ports, here, and then unload them on the way back. Which way is this steamer bound?" he asked the man at the wheel.

"For Jamaica, sah; I guess, maastah," that ebony worthy replied. "It's too loaded down fo' to be teckin' bananas to de States."

"That's so; I might have thought of that. Of course it has heavier freight aboard than bananas, or else it would ride further out of the water." Then, taking up his field-glass, which was by him, he added, —

"Why, it's the 'Ailsa'; I wonder whether my good friends, Captain Morris and Purser Monks, are still on board of her? I hope our skipper will be back in time for me to take the small-boat and row over and see."

As he spoke he glanced towards the shore and saw that the skipper was already on his way back. As soon as he arrived, they arranged to be rowed over to the "Ailsa," but a short distance away, and they were there by the time that the long-boat had come out from the island with its cargo of negro stevedores. Captain Morris, a short, jovial, elderly man, every inch of him the capable captain and thorough English gentleman, and Purser Monks, as jolly a mixture of hard worker on deck and good fellow on shore as ever trod an Atlas Line vessel,—and that is saying much,—were heartily surprised and glad to see the Doctor, who, they said, was always turning up in the most unexpected places. They told him he and his young companions had better come direct with them to Jamaica, where they would be in two days; but, with a handshake and a promise to try to see them in that island, by the time they had made another trip, our party said good-bye and ran down the rope ladder just after the last darkey had come aboard. And in a few moments the "Ailsa" was steaming on her way, and but a little while later was only represented by a long trail of smoke on the horizon.

About noon the next day they came to anchor in the harbor of Great Inagua Island, the time of their trip from Fortune Island having been used to finish the division of their belongings into two sets of parcels,—those which were to go with them and those that were now all ready to be shipped north by the next steamer. Here they bade their skipper and his crew good-bye, supplementing the very modest payment exacted for their trip from Nassau by gifts of knives, pipes, and other trifles, which gave great pleasure.

On shore they found that the next north-bound vessel was not expected for five or six days, but that a small schooner was expected to sail for Tortuga in two days. At once they put their homeward-bound freight in charge of the gentleman who filled the complex rôle of steamship agent, contractor for stevedores, agent for several marine insurance companies, grower and shipper of produce and fruit for northern markets, and general manager for every one around him, besides filling the honorable position of resident representative of Her Majesty's Government and Consular Agent for the United States; and then they engaged passage for Tortuga, agreeing to come on board of their new vessel in the evening of the second day following, so as to be prepared for an early start the next morning.

Although they had a cordial invitation from the gentleman of many duties, whose heart was as large as his executive capacity, to be his guests, they decided to hire a boatman to take them to a deserted part of the shore, where they could enjoy the camper's life with entire freedom and could give all their attention to their collecting. At the point selected, so used to the outdoor life did they already feel, things went on very smoothly, without any of the excitement that made "Camp Flamingo" and "Camp Octopus," as Harry had named them, so memorable.

On the morning of their last day there, however, Harry had an experience that was likely to be remembered, and that the Doctor cautioned them both they must take to heart as teaching a useful lesson.

They had had a splendid morning's collecting, and were on their way back to camp for lunch, when Harry, putting his hand into the pocket where he kept butterflies folded in papers, quickly took it out again, with a cry of pain. The Doctor was the first to see that there were a dozen or more small bright red ants causing his agony, and quickly pulling off the boy's coat he dropped it on the ground, and then saturated the bitten hand with alcohol, which quicker than anything else would kill or drive his tormentors away, although for a moment it did add somewhat to his suffering. Then, turning his attention to the coat, the Doctor quickly turned the pocket inside out, with his forceps, pouring from it twenty or twenty-five of what had been papers containing butterflies, but which now were simply tattered paper and torn wings, the bodies of each one having entirely disappeared. With this mess there came out a few crumbs of Graham wafers, and these the Doctor knew at once to be the cause of all the trouble. Harry, who had no little trouble keeping the tears back, so great was the pain in his swollen hand, confessed that he had had three or four wafers in that pocket, "just to nibble at," when he started out, but that he had no idea the ants would find them, and in such a short time as they must have had while he sat down on the ground just for a moment.

"There is no telling where or when ants will appear on

the scene in the tropics, and they are so voracious, and in such enormous numbers, that it is never safe to trust to anything but ceaseless caution. Besides your pain, you have lost a lot of valuable butterflies, as to-day's collecting was about the best we have had. So, you see, it pays to remember ants and all sorts of creeping things in this part of the world."

"I don't believe all those butterflies are ruined," said Ned, dropping to his knees on the ground, where the Doctor had emptied Harry's pocket, and beginning to sort the papers over; "and, for my part, I think there is a lot of fuss being made over a bite or two from some tiny ants."

No sooner was this out of his mouth than he yelled out,—

"Jumping grasshoppers! but those little red scamps have hot feet," and, suiting his actions to his words, he jumped back as far as he could, and began violently brushing off his right hand. Then he continued: "I beg your pardon, Hal; I had no idea they were such biters. Only two or three got on me from the first paper I picked up, but that is quite enough for my curiosity."

On the way back, as Harry's hand decreased in painfulness, he said:—

"Are all parts of the tropics as bad as this with such pests? Shall we have to watch for them this way everywhere?"

"Most parts are far worse," was the reply. "I have had the pleasure to find, on my arrival at my camp on the upper Amazon River, after a tiresome but productive day's collecting, that on my way home minute ants had even succeeded in climbing up my back, on to my tin collecting-box, that seemed well-nigh water-tight, wedged their way inside, and, as I trudged home, congratulating myself on the rare species captured, were at that very moment tearing them wing from wing."

"How do you account for the little demons finding out so soon where there is food, and so soon having a whole army on hand to help them?" asked Ned.

"In the case of those that crawled from my back into the box, it was largely accidental," the Doctor replied. "I had, doubtless, knocked them off of trees and bushes on myself as I passed. In Harry's case, he had, in all probability, sat down near a nest or a foraging party of considerable size. While he was there, they were quick to detect the presence of the Graham wafers in his pocket, and this they did by means of their highly developed sense of smell. This, as Sir John Lubbock, the foremost English student of ant life, has shown, is situated mainly in their antennæ. By delicate experiments he and others have proved that insects, and especially ants, that were excessively acute in detecting certain odors at some distance, were far less so, and required much more time, if deprived of their antennæ."

"Why, I have read somewhere that insects' feelers were used in hearing," said Ned.

"So some naturalists contend," the Doctor replied, "and perhaps with perfect right. You are both too familiar with the laws of sight and sound for me to need to do more than remind you that sounds are produced by sound waves of different length or duration, — a dull, heavy sound being the product of fewer waves to the given time, and a high-pitched one to a much greater number of waves in the same period. Now, as you are also well aware, light is also the product of waves, the length of the light waves determining the color in the rainbow. But in between the very highest rate of waves that produce sounds that our ears are capable of hearing, and the lowest that produce light that we are capable of seeing, there is a vast range of wave lengths that make no perceptible impression upon us, whatever. Yet there are excellent reasons, based on some careful mechanical experiments, for believing that these intermediate waves do make an impression on some insects, and perhaps all; and that it is through the antennæ that these impressions are carried to their tiny brains."

Late that afternoon they went on board their vessel, after writing and mailing letters home, laden with accounts of their daily doings, and after declining the kind invitation of the consular agent, who, Harry said, was "a whole four-horse team, and a little dog under the wagon, besides," to stay over and take part in catching some wild horses that range the rich and ample savannahs, or grass plains, of the island. The next morning when they got on deck, they were out of sight of Great Inagua, and the morning after, when they came on deck, they were just making a harbor in the island of Tortuga. There they left their new skipper, and here they were on Haitian soil, and for the first time away from an English-speaking country. As they planned their coming tour through "the Black

Republic," they could see to the south the beautiful mountains of Northern Haiti and imagine themselves a party of the freebooters of two centuries before, who made this island their favorite meeting-place.

CHAPTER VIII

THE EARLY HOME OF THE FREEBOOTERS

A Mulatto Landlady — The Multitudes of Blacks — The Early Natives — The Buccaneers — National Hypocrisy — The True Discoverer — Late Views of Columbus — Ant Cows — Herders and Protectors of Caterpillars — Ants versus Wasps — An Alligator's Nest — Luring an Alligator — Full of Fight — Ho! for Haiti — Flying Machines and their Future

AS they intended to remain at Tortuga but a day, the Doctor thought it hardly worth while for them to pitch their tent and unpack their camp outfit for so short a time; and therefore they found board, comfortable if rather primitive, at the house of an elderly dame who was of that uncertain yellow complexion which their friend, Professor Watson, would have called "African blonde." This was the boys' first experience in living in a negro household, and with characteristic American squeamishness they felt far from contented with the arrangement at the first. But the Doctor soon explained to them, that in their own northern home they thought nothing of eating the food prepared by a colored cook, and nothing of sleeping in a bed made by a colored chambermaid; then, he very logically asked, why should they object to the same things simply because they found them in a house owned by a colored woman.

"If you young men," he concluded, "aspire to become thorough naturalists and explorers, you must put aside all these foolish race prejudices and make the best of things as they come to you. And I can assure you that if you will try to do this you will soon come to regard the disposition and comparative refinement of your landlady or passing acquaintance, and not their skin or geographical origin. In my own case I have numbered some of my best and most trusted friends among men of African descent."

"How has it come that all these islands are so thickly settled with black and brown people now, Doctor, and that there are so few whites and no trace of the original Indian inhabitants?" Ned asked.

"I have already explained to you how rapidly the cruel and inhuman methods adopted by the early Spaniards towards the natives of these islands caused them to be practically depopulated in a generation or two. Columbus estimated that there were 60,000 Arrawaks, the most peaceable of all the native Americans, living in Jamaica when he discovered it. Yet, in less than twenty-five years, it was estimated that only 3000 remained. They had been worked to death in the mines or on the plantations, and those who would not submit to this slavery were in thousands of cases put to death. Of course when the Indians began to grow scarce and the need for laborers increased with every year's increase in Spanish settlement, it became necessary to look elsewhere for aid, and it was the most natural thing to turn to Africa, and bring to these islands that willing, generally docile, hardship-enduring people. They had been used to slavery in their own land for centuries, and bad as it was, American slavery was not as bad as that they had known in their own barbarous homes. As a consequence they throve and multiplied, while the Indian, who had never felt restraint before and could not brook slavery, soon pined away and left the land to his more enduring black rival."

"Were all the natives of these islands so very peaceable? Were there not some warlike ones among them?" asked Harry.

"Columbus and other writers speak of the Caribs, found in Haiti and other islands to the south, as very fierce and bloodthirsty, and we know that they were much dreaded by the other islanders and that they were cannibals. It is thought by some that the word *cannibal* is derived from the name *Carib*. There are no longer any Caribs left in the West Indies, although some half-breeds claim to be such. Years ago their scattered remnants were moved by the British government to Honduras, where a considerable number of them still live between the Patook River and Belize. They still retain something of their language and customs."

"Who were the buccaneers, of whom we often read, Doctor? Were they natives or Europeans, mostly?" asked Ned.

"After Spain had thoroughly possessed herself of these islands, she became very tyrannical and oppressive, and, especially among the English, French, and Dutch settlers who had been attracted here, there grew up a hatred for her misrule and oppression, which finally broke out in open rebellion and lawlessness. The few natives then left were very skilful in preserving meat by fire and smoke in their little smoke-houses, called, in their language, 'boucans.' The Spanish government placed a heavy tax on all butchering and exacted a heavy license from all who sold the cured meats brought from Spain, and, therefore, a secret trade in this native-made 'boucanned' meat sprang up. The adventurers who rebelled against the authority of Spain learned this trade from the natives, and they became adepts in this illegal butcher trade, which paid no tax to Spain, and were soon known far and wide as 'boucanners,' which, as you can see, was easily changed into *buccaneers*.

"In time more serious things than the meat trade were made the excuse for the lawlessness that these men practised, and in a little while, when Protestant England fitted out piratical expeditions to take the power in these islands from Catholic Spain, religion became the avowed motive, although the old name for the native butchers remained. In time the Dutch name *frie-boter*, 'free plunderer,' was used instead, and from it we get our word *freebooter*. The records of these men, as set forth in the writings of Father Labat, John Oexmelic (commonly called Esquemeling), and others, read more like the wildest tales of imagination than the truth; but those were strange days, and these waters we are now looking upon have seen sights never again to be seen in this world. This island of Tortuga was the chief seat of power and of warfare for the freebooters for over a hundred years, and there are few spots of its size anywhere in the world that have seen an equal amount of bloodshed in the same space of time."

"How did it come about, Doctor, that these islands, which, I have read, Spain took possession of so as to convert them to the Christian religion, were for so many years the places where so much wickedness and murder went on?"

"Spain, like all other lands of that time, and this time as well, made the conversion of native peoples the excuse for acquiring new lands from which she hoped to take gold and precious stones. She, as a nation, cared nothing whatever for the souls of the poor wretches she conquered. You may see the same thing to-day. In the name of Christianity England uses Gatling and Maxim guns to plough down the Zulus, Matabeles, and the natives beyond Sikkim Pass; Germany in Zanzibar and in the Cameroon territory does the same; and France in Siam, and Belgium on the Congo, have no better record. Our own land is the only one of the Great Powers that has not this sin to answer for.

"Nothing shows how hollow were the pretences of Spain," the Doctor continued, "better than Columbus's own words. Writing of these islands to his sovereigns in Spain, he said: 'This country excels all others as far as the day surpasses the night in splendor; the natives love their neighbors as themselves; their conversation is the sweetest imaginable; their faces always smiling; and so gentle and affectionate are they, that I swear to your highnesses there is not a better people in the world.' Yet almost before the children of these people he so highly praised had grown to manhood, all had practically perished from off the earth, owing to the slavery and tortures which he devised and set to work. It was a sad day for these simple islanders when the first sight of their land was caught by Rodrigo de Triana."

"Triana! Why, I thought Columbus himself discovered the land," said Harry.

"There had been a reward of 10,000 marivedis as an annual pension offered by the Spanish crown to the man who first saw land, and when Columbus saw that this sum, which was only about $30 in our money, was to go to Triana, who first called out the land that night, at 2 A.M., he claimed to have seen a flickering light moving back and forth some hours before, and on the strength of that claim kept the money for himself, although he was to be made by his discoveries one of the wealthiest men of his time."

That afternoon they took a stroll along one of the roads leading into the interior of the island, finally following a trail into a jungle of thick tropical growth, where the Doctor told them they were likely to find rare beetles, because some one had been chopping down some timber, and beetles dearly love the neighborhood of piles of bark and fresh chips. As they were walking along, poking into a heap on one hand, and examining the flowers of some plant on the other, Harry suddenly exclaimed:—

"Come here, quick, Doctor! See what I've found. Hundreds of these pestiferous ants eating up some sort of caterpillar. No wonder butterflies are so scarce here, if that's what becomes of their young ones!"

"Slowly, my boy. Don't jump at conclusions," the Doctor said, as he and Ned joined Harry at the side of a tall *Cassia*, or false sensitive-plant, whereon scores of ants were rapidly running from place to place, among a large colony of small caterpillars. "Be sure you see one of the ants doing a caterpillar any harm, before you charge, try, and hang them as murderers! Here, take this large magnifying-glass and see what you can see through that."

Harry, feeling from the Doctor's words that he had made some error in his first judgment, carefully bent over one of the leaves on which there were many of both kinds of insects, and for some moments did not utter a word. When, at last, he did speak, he had a very different verdict to render.

"This tropical country is the queerest place I ever dreamt of. I'll be switched if those ants don't walk up to the caterpillars and pat them on the backs with their feelers, and the caterpillars show no signs of worry or fear at all. I can't see what makes them such good friends; but there don't seem to be any signs of their being enemies."

"You take the glass, Ned, and see whether you can see any reason for this seeming friendship," was the Doctor's only comment.

This the other boy did, examining several of the leaves and their tiny inhabitants with the greatest care. Finally he tried to drive the ants from one of the leaves with his finger, but the quick way in which he withdrew it showed that the bond of friendship between the two very different insects was such as to call for aggressive measures on the part of the ants.

"My, how those little rascals can bite!" he said, shaking his finger. "I can only see what Hal saw; plenty of signs of affection on the part of the ants, and entire indifference on the part of the caterpillars, who go right on feeding. But I can't see any cause for such strange antics."

"Hal, take this smaller glass," the Doctor said; "you will have to get closer to the leaf, and will not see so big an area at once; but it is more powerful than the other. Now I will tell you both what to look for, and I think then you will understand this performance, which is one of the most interesting in the insect world. Now look at one of the caterpillars, and you will see that near the hinder end of each, and right on top, there are little tubes projecting upwards, and then you will notice that it is always to this end that the ant approaches with its pats and caresses. Watch one of the ants very carefully, now. Doesn't it pat with its antennæ, or feelers, right on or around those tubes? Now, watch the upper end of the tube, and I'll wager that you'll each see a little drop of a honey-yellow fluid appear there; and it will then be easy enough, when you see the ant carefully suck up all this fluid and run off to repeat the performance with another caterpillar, to understand what the bond of friendship is. For these caterpillars are simply the cows of the ants, and the thick, gummy, and very sweet fluid which then exudes from those tiny tubes is a sort of honey-milk on which these ants mainly subsist, and their antennæ are simply used in this way to milk their caterpillar cattle."

As the Doctor finished speaking, both boys looked up from the colonies of caterpillars they had been watching, and Ned eagerly asked,—

"But where do the 'cows' come in? I can see that this is very nice for the ants, but I don't see what the caterpillars gain by it all."

"If you boys will find me two or three 'lady-bugs,' or other specimens of the *Coccinelidæ* family of beetles, I will soon prove to you that the caterpillars are even greater gainers than the ants by this friendship," the Doctor replied. And as they went off, looking over the leaves and twigs of bushes for what they wanted, he deftly picked some of the caterpillars off of the leaves with his forceps, and deposited them in a pill-box, which he placed in his pocket.

In a few moments each of the boys was back with two or three lady-bugs; and taking one of these the Doctor carefully dropped it into the pill-box in which were the caterpillars, holding it so that both boys could watch the result. No sooner had the beetle touched the bottom of the box than it grabbed one of the caterpillars, and fastening its hard jaws in the fleshy sides of the helpless creature, began to extract the life juices from it. Then taking another beetle, he carefully held it over a leaf whereon there were a large number of caterpillars being guarded by a score or more of ants, and gently dropped it. Again the beetle made a rush for a caterpillar, but it was not so quick as a dozen ants, which rushed for it and began so savagely attacking it, that the poor lady-bug, after trying to fly away with its burden of biting and tearing ants, relinquished its hold upon the leaf and rolled to the ground, where it was no better off, as Harry discovered, reporting that the ants were tearing it to pieces while he watched them with the glass. This experiment the Doctor tried several times, and in each case the result was the same, save in one, where the lady-bug, evidently knowing what to expect, quickly flew away before the ants could reach it, and without paying any attention to the caterpillars.

"How long do you think this species of caterpillar, which is that of the beautiful little sky-blue butterfly, *Lycæna marina*, of which we have caught so many fine specimens, would last if they did not have the ants to defend them?" the Doctor asked.

"Not very long, I am sure!" Ned replied. "This is really the most wonderful thing. Why don't we have such wonderful species at home, Doctor? why are they all in the warm countries?"

"They are not," was the reply. "There are two species of this same genus of butterflies in your State, which are thus shielded from harm by ants, and there are a number of species of plant-lice and of tree-hoppers that are also protected in the same way. It is common everywhere, yet there are few who observe so carefully as ever to have seen it. I have been wondering for some days that neither of you has seen this before; for, now that it is known to you, you will find it occurring on every hand."

"Why didn't you tell us of it?" asked Harry. "We might never have seen it."

"All I propose to do is to teach you how to observe, take you where you can observe, and help you to understand what you have observed. If I were to keep pointing out all the new things for you, you would soon fall into the habit of depending on me. Then you would grow unobserving, and, in a certain sense, indolent. Don't forget the flamingoes, and the two brave hunters with only dust-shot in their guns! Of course, I will not let you leave a locality where there is something to be seen, that you can see nowhere else, without pointing it out; but otherwise you will have to wait to find things out with your own observing powers. These are already remarkably good, considering your years and experience; but they will now improve rapidly with constant use."

"Do the leaf-hoppers that receive this care from the ants give them honey in the same way?" asked Harry.

"Yes, much the same; only more of it. The 'honey-dew' which is so often found on trees and shrubs in great quantities, in the early mornings, and which the honey-bees seek so eagerly for their use, is the product of these and the plant-lice. The mother tree-hopper deposits her eggs in little clusters in a cottony nest, and over this she stands guard, until her young are hatched. Then her instinct tells her that it is safe to leave them to the care of the ants, and she does so. The ants may be found guarding them in every stage, from the tiny newly hatched, to the nearly grown individual, about ready to get wings. In some cases I have observed wasps, which are as fond of this honey as are the ants, trying to possess themselves of it; but as they dare not light on the leaf, for fear a horde of ants will grapple with them and inflict deadly bites, they attempt to brush all the ants away by flying repeatedly at them, and brushing them off with their legs. But as there are endless reinforcements of the ants, the wasp usually gives up the job as too much for him."

On their way home they came back by the shores of a lagoon or salt-water pond, and the Doctor cautioned them to proceed very carefully, as they might be able to see an alligator. This was a promise of such big and exciting game, that one word of caution was all that was necessary, and they tiptoed their way along, hardly daring to breathe, and taking the utmost care to escape all dead sticks or other objects that would make a noise and announce their presence.

Suddenly the Doctor, who was in the lead, stopped, and pointing to a pile of dead sticks and leaves at one side, said in a whisper that it was a last season's nest, but of course was empty now. So they found it, but they could see that it had been carefully made, and was not a mere drift-pile, as they at first thought. But there were no alligators in sight, look as carefully as they might; at least, so both the boys assured the Doctor.

"I brought a couple of alligator eggs along in my game-pocket," the Doctor said. "Our landlady lent them to me, and I thought we might be glad to have them along, as they are the best sort of alligator bait, as you shall see." Saying which, he took out of his pocket two eggs somewhat larger than a hen's egg, and of a very rough, porcelain-like surface and thick shell, that had been blown. Taking one of these in each hand, he began rubbing them violently together, making a hollow sound something like the clashing together of broken plates, at the same time saying, —

"Watch the water over the other side, there, near that floating log."

At the very first sound, the old, water-soaked piece of timber, that was floating so deep as to be scarcely visible, turned directly towards them, and, much to the astonishment of the boys, began to approach rapidly. In a few moments it had crossed the pond, and by the time it was ready to come out on the shore, the boys saw that it had the bulging eyes and saw-toothed back of an alligator, and was a much more formidable object than a stick of wood. As it came out upon the sand, the Doctor advanced toward it, with a heavy stick of wood in his right hand, slipping the eggs into his pocket again as he did so.

"An alligator on shore is most dangerous with its tail," he remarked to the boys, who stayed behind, watching him eagerly. "Although this one is only about eight feet long, she could, probably, break my legs, should she get a chance at them with a swish of her tail. Of course that mouth of hers would soon dispose of me in the water, by dragging me down under the surface and holding me there until I was drowned; but on land it is very easy to dodge it. With the tail, however, they are wonderously quick, and it is dangerous business getting within its reach."

As he was saying this, he advanced slowly towards the hideous-looking creature, which lay quietly facing him at the edge of the water, showing no signs of life other than one gap, which displayed a terrible array of teeth in a mouth that appeared to be quite one-third its whole length. Whether it realized that alligator eggs were out of season, or whether it saw something dangerous in the Doctor's eyes, it did not wait for him to get to it, but turning slowly, slid off into the water.

"Well, she was a coward!" laughed the Doctor. "But that wouldn't end quite so pleasantly on some Amazonian waters, for instance. There, I once found a nest with seventeen eggs in it, and though I handled them with the greatest care, — for I did not care to attract the mother, — I knocked two of them together slightly, and in a jiffy was confronted with an alligator over fifteen feet long and as full of fight as a cross bull. Fortunately I had a rifle with me; so its skin is now in the Museum at Berlin."

"What do they make nests for? they don't sit on their eggs to hatch them, do they?" asked Harry.

"No, they depend on the sun's heat; but the nest serves to raise the eggs from the damp ground and, no doubt, the leaves add to the heat by their decaying. They usually lay about twenty eggs, and it is safe to say that where there is a nest there is always a mother alligator near enough to hear the peculiar noise made by the eggs rubbing together. Many animals like alligators' eggs; some monkeys take them up into trees and drop them so far that they break, after which they descend and eat the contents. But it takes a crafty and quick animal to get away with more than one from a nest before the watchful mother appears."

"Are alligators' eggs eaten by men?" asked Harry.

"Very frequently, and many people like them. I do not; they are too oily or greasy. As to alligator flesh, that is abominable. I have had to eat it several times when there was no other animal food to take its place;

but I have never been able to learn to like it, for it is very rank and muddy in taste. But on the Orinoco and upper Amazon the natives highly prize it at certain seasons. They hold the fattest pieces over the fire, each man being his own cook, and turn them until very well done."

The next morning, bright and early, they set sail for the near-by coast of Haiti, which was plainly in sight, the tall, well-wooded, rounded hills presenting a fine contrast to the flat and sandy islands among which they had been sailing.

"This seems to be a case," Ned suddenly remarked, when they were about half there, "when a flying-machine or a balloon would be a handy thing to have. With the wind in our favor, as it now is, we would be able to get across here in short order, in a balloon."

"The recent discoveries of Professor Langley, director of our National Museum at Washington, and of Mr. Maxim, the inventor of the machine-gun that fires so rapidly, indicate that in a very few years we shall be in possession of a flying-engine or machine at least capable of carrying two or three persons," the Doctor said. "But there will be no balloon about it. A receptacle large enough to hold the gas required for a safe ascension is far too big to be manageable in a stiff wind; at best it can only drift with the air current. But our inventors are just on the verge of perfecting the details of machines whereby we shall fly on the same principle as do the birds, although we shall need to have such light artificial power to aid us as will come from a small electric dynamo or an oil engine. Nature has not made flying birds to weigh over thirty-five pounds, and there are physical impossibilities believed to be in the way of man flying by his own unaided strength. The principles on which such flying will be possible are now well understood and are very simple; what we now wait for is the perfection of mechanical details that will put these principles into use. But I venture to predict that before you boys are beyond young manhood or before this century is ended, in all probability, flying-machines will be no more of an innovation than were bicycles fifteen years ago."

CHAPTER IX

THE BLACK REPUBLIC

A Glimpse at Haitian History — The Most Degraded Land in Christendom — A Study in Human Government — An Old Friend — Elisha — A Dark View of Haiti — Vaudoux Witchcraft — "Haiti," its Derivation and Spelling — A Creole Dinner — An Array of Fruit — "Matrimony" — A Pet Lizard

THAT afternoon, after the boys had lunched at the hotel in Port à Paix, the Doctor proposed that they take a stroll along the coast road and collect, while he gave them a brief insight into the history of the country in which they expected to spend the next two or three weeks. This they readily assented to; for already they were filled with curiosity to know something of a people whose life, conversation, and manners appeared to be so different from any with which they were yet acquainted. When, after walking some distance out of the town, and having attracted much curiosity from the natives by their nets and collecting-outfit, they came to a stretch of country where there seemed to be no one to annoy or overhear them, the Doctor told them something of Haitian history.

"The Spaniards having converted all the natives on the island of Hispaniola, by working them to death in their mines and plantations, filled their places with countless hordes of African slaves, who, having been used to slavery for centuries in their own country, were of tougher constitution. For nearly two hundred years the Spanish colonies on this island throve, cities grew, mammoth estates were cultivated, and Santo Domingo, as the island had come to be known, was justly considered the richest spot in the Western World. Then the western and most valuable half of the island was taken from the Spaniards by the buccaneers and became the French province of Haiti. When the French Revolution broke out, slavery could not be allowed to remain as a blot in French dominions, and the blacks, then more than two-thirds of the inhabitants, were freed and declared citizens. Immediately the blacks signalled their coming into freedom by the massacre of the whole French population — men, women, and children.

"Napoleon sent here an army to overpower the negro hordes, most of whom had no knowledge beyond that of hoeing cane or making sugar, and none whatever of warfare. These took to their heels, and while they hid in the impassable jungles of the interior mountains the deadly yellow fever fought their battles for them and finally forced the then unconquered Napoleon to admit that the Haitian climate was greater than he, and that he could not afford to send here tens of thousands of troops to die before they had ever caught sight of the enemy. France having given up all hope of regaining control over her colony, both England and Spain tried their hands at conquering it; but they, too, soon saw that the cake was not worth the penny, although they were both anxious to re-enslave the blacks here, because they feared the effect of a large country filled with free blacks so near their slave-holding colonies of Jamaica and Cuba. This was about one hundred years ago, and I cannot sum up the outcome of the bloody century just ending better than to quote the words of Mr. James Anthony Froude, the great historian."

Taking a book from his pocket, the Doctor read as follows : —

"Haiti has thus for nearly a century been a black independent state. The negro race have had it to themselves and have not been interfered with. They were equipped when they started on their career of freedom with the Catholic religion, a civilized language, European laws and manners, and the knowledge of various arts and occupations which they had learnt while they were slaves. They speak French still; they are nominally Catholics still; and the tags and rags of the gold lace of French civilization continue to cling about their institutions. But in the heart of them has revived the old idolatry of the Gold Coast, and in the villages of the interior, where they are out of sight and can follow their instincts, they sacrifice children in the serpent's honor after the manner of their forefathers. Perhaps nothing could be expected from a liberty which was inaugurated by assassination and plunder. Political changes which prove successful do not begin in that way."

"During the century just past," continued the Doctor, "Haiti has seen nearly fifty different rebellions, and she has only known peace when some one of the number, stronger in mind than the others, has seized upon the presidential office and become a tyrant who put to death all who dared to breathe a word opposed to him. And that sort of enforced peace has only lasted as long as his combined enemies have been prevented from putting a stop to his rule by the aid of the poisoned cup or stiletto. Then they have gone to work again quarrelling among themselves. The land in which we are now going to live for a little while can truthfully be charged with having seen more useless bloodshed and savage crime than any other in the Western Hemisphere. So, too, it is safe to say that to-day it is the most degraded and most hopelessly wicked land in Christendom.

"Your father and I agreed that it would be worth while for you to spend some time here, both on account of its rich natural history and its remarkable population. Ever since our late war in the States, what is known as 'the negro question' has been of prime importance in our government; and it seems to bid fair to grow in importance for some time to come. In no way can you better obtain a just idea of how the negro must not be treated or allowed to treat himself, and of how he should be, than by first seeing this island and then visiting Jamaica. Here we shall see the black, freed from all white government, going down to the depths of superstition and idolatry; there we shall see the same people prospering under the council and aid of the whites. It is, therefore, that most important species of the mammal family, Man, *Homo sapiens*, to which we are to give our principal attention here.

"But you must always remember that it is not safe to seem too curious about the doings of these people; for they are very suspicious of the whites, and, without doubt, there will be some in the interior, where we shall soon go, who would quickly resent our regarding them as an interesting study. We must seem to make butterfly-hunting our first and only motive for being here; and, especially, you must carefully refrain from laughing at them or their ways, unless you are sure they want to be laughed at."

"What do you mean, when you say they would resent our studying them, Doctor? How would they resent it?" asked Ned.

"They have a very wholesome dread of the United States, and therefore there would be no danger of any criminal act against us near the coast. But I do not for one moment doubt that there are scores of ignorant blacks a little way back in the mountains who would not hesitate one moment to poison our food or our water in retaliation for any fancied slight or injury."

"Gracious! I guess this is a pretty good island to dodge; it looks to me as though we'd have done better to take the 'Ailsa' at Fortune Island and go straight on to Jamaica," said Harry, with a nervous laugh.

"By no means," the Doctor replied. "You boys have the full use of your minds; you have good memories, a fair control of your faces, and ought to know when to mind your own affairs. This part of our trip will not only be very useful to you, for the reason already explained, but it will be an excellent training in some of the more difficult features of an explorer's life, teaching the very useful lesson of how to get along comfortably with very uncomfortable people. I have been studying you young men with the utmost care, and I would not have brought you here had I not felt sure that you were quite equal to doing as well as any one under the circumstances. I shall write to your father to-night and assure him that, as I am so sure you are the stuff of which true explorers and naturalists are made, I start on the Haitian part of our trip with perfect confidence."

"Well, I guess after that send-off we can't help but do our best," said Ned. "You are a good deal like our teacher of mathematics at school, Doctor. He puts us on our best behavior by telling us that if we can't do a thing, no class can, and we always get it done, it seems. You needn't worry about our being all eyes and ears, without these suspicious Haitians ever guessing it. We'll show the Doctor how we can do the great 'Hawkshaw, the detective' act, won't we, Hal?"

"Indeed we will; and now is a good time to begin, I guess. That black fellow over there has been watching us for about ten minutes in a very queer way, Doctor," Harry replied.

Looking in the direction indicated, the Doctor had no more than taken in the squat form and broad black face of their new-found spy, when he smiled and shouted: —

"Hello, Dave! Why, this is good luck to see you here! Why, man, I thought you were living in the States." As he said this he advanced quickly, and meeting the negro half-way, shook him warmly by the hand. Then, turning to the boys, he said: —

"Ned, Harry, this is Mr. David Benton, of Savannah, Georgia. Dave, these are the two young Masters Dawson who are taking a trip with me, collecting butterflies and all such things, just as you remember I like to do. Boys, you remember that only yesterday I told you that among my many good friends in different parts of the world I numbered some black ones among the best of them. Dave, here, is one of the very best of the best, and it does me good to see his fat, jolly face again. Say, you old sea-dog, what are you doing down here?" he added, turning again to the negro, who stood by with twinkling eyes and a mammoth grin.

"Well, yo' see, Massah Doctah, dat my ole 'oman didn't tak no shine to de State of Georgy, and nowhere we moved seemed like it suited her nohow. So when I see dat she begin a'pinin' and a'sorrowin' fer dis yer home islan' o' hers, I jes' packed up all our vallebuls and came down yer to lib. It don' mek no great odds to me whar I lib, an' I allus did say, 'please de ladies' all de time, if yo' want peace and happiness in des yer wo'ld." Then with a scrape of the foot and a duck of the head that showed plainer than words his origin in the States, he added: "But I is sho' 'nough glad to see yo' down yer a'catchin' all sorts o' crawlin' things agin, an' I 'ud be might'ly honored fer to heb yo' all come to de house for a lil' while."

From the conversation that followed, the boys gathered that Dave had been a sailor on a vessel sailing between Savannah and the West Indies for over twenty years, starting in his early boyhood. Becoming acquainted with the Doctor, on one of the latter's trips to these islands, he had left a seafaring life, and for four years had been his guide, assistant, and general factotum. Coming to Haiti, he fell in love with one of the belles of Port à Paix, and married her here, and after some years spent on a little place on the Georgia coast, bought with his savings, had come back here, where he was now engaged in the dual life of fisherman and market-gardener. Furthermore, the Doctor soon found out that Dave would not want any better job, for a couple of weeks or so, than to act as guide, cook, and interpreter to the party while they remained in the island.

"Bress my soul, Massah Doctah," he cried, "but won' 'Lisha be more dan glad to see yo'! Yass, sah, I'se got 'Lisha yet, and he yain't no diff'unt from de way he was de day yo' las' set eyes on him."

"Elisha," said Harry; "who is he? Is he your son?"

"Well, I s'pose yo' might call him dat, fo' he's de on'y chile me an' Hortense is got. But he yain't much fo' to call pretty, fo' a son. He do hab a mos' awdacious mouf and he am about de bowleggedes' critter eber yo' see," was the reply, with a jolly laugh, that appeared to illustrate that Elisha, if he was a son, came very naturally by his "awdacious mouf."

When, after a walk of nearly a mile back towards the town, they arrived at a small frame cottage, standing back in a cluster of mango trees and oleander bushes and a great tamarind tree waving over all, with neatly kept walks and flower beds, in great contrast to the untidiness of most of the houses around, Dave turned in, and with another of his profound bows asked them to be seated on the porch while he went to call Hortense and Elisha. Just as he disappeared Harry shouted, —

"Look out, Doctor! Here comes a giant bull dog!" Saying which he quickly jumped up on the railing, where he was promptly followed by Ned. But their fright was unnecessary, as they soon saw, when the Doctor whistled to the villainous-looking brute, whose enormous body, short, bowed legs, horrible jaw, and a bald patch on his head as a reminder of a former fight, made up a most forbidding combination, and called him by his name "Elisha." The boys were much amused at Dave's sense of humor in alluding to this brute as his only child, and asked the Doctor how such an odd name had been given to him.

"That you must get Dave to tell you; I can't do it justice. The dog belonged on the vessel that Dave used to sail on, and when he came to leave it, Dave was so loth to leave the dog, then known as Nero, that I bought it for him."

After Dave had returned with his wife, Hortense, a rather fine-looking mulatto woman, who remembered the Doctor and greeted him pleasantly and with much grace, Ned asked, —

"How did you come to call that dog Elisha, Mr. Benton?"

"Don' Mr. Benton me; eberybody jes' calls me Dave, an' dat's de name I like bes'. Dat dawg? Oh, yo' see dat bal' spot on his head? Well, he's mighty sore on dat spot, an' yo' don' want to tech upon it, 'less yo' know him mighty good. So, yo' see, he's jes' like dat udder ole bal' head what we read about in de Scriptu'es; it yaint safe to boddah him about his bal' head, an' so I jes' call him ''Lisha.'"

The boys soon found this quaint reasoning was a constant thing with Dave, and it was easy to see why he had been so acceptable a companion to Doctor Bartlett. So entertained were they with the man's endless flow of odd humor combined with rare common sense, that it was nearly dark when they finally said good-bye, promising to call the following evening to take dinner with Dave and Hortense.

"Shall we really take our dinner there, Doctor?" said Ned, doubtfully.

"Certainly. In no better way can you become used to what is called Creole cooking, and it will be a very good introduction to the sort of living you may expect when we are not camping out. Everything will be scrupulously clean, and you will have no trouble to forget that you are not eating at an Anglo-Saxon table, where in many cases, you would not find as good cooking or as neat service."

That night, as they sat on the piazza of their boarding-house, they were joined by a Catholic priest, and a French merchant of the town, and the talk naturally drifted to the condition of Haiti and its outlook for improvement. From this conversation, to which the boys were eager listeners, they learned that the priest felt much discouraged, fearing that the heathen superstitions which the negroes had inherited from their African parents and grandparents were so deeply rooted in their natures as to make it impossible to civilize them. The Frenchman, however, who had lived in Jamaica and in Barbadoes, believed that, if ruled fairly and kindly by whites until they learned to understand and appreciate the advantages of laws and an orderly life, they would prove to be a civilized people and a credit to their race. But he agreed with the priest that they were going back into barbarity in Haiti, where white example and white influence were sadly needed, and thought that they did not, as a people, know what religion or morals really meant, for the one who prayed the most, or offered the most freely to the Saints, would steal the most or be the first to take a false oath against his neighbor.

Both agreed that public honor was unknown to the Haitians, and that none of them considered it wrong to steal from the State. While that was so, every new election was sure to be followed by revolutions on the part of the defeated party, who were only anxious to be in power so as to get a chance at the public treasury. While the country was nominally a Catholic one, it was in reality largely idolatrous. The worship of the snake, known here as Vaudoux, and in the English colonies as Obeah, the oldest known form of religion, and that alluded to when Moses erected a serpent in the wilderness, was daily gaining ground, and the priest of God was no longer as powerful as the priest of Ob, the all-powerful snake.

As to self-government and the honest use of the ballot, on which all true republics must depend, they neither knew what that meant nor did they care to know. In a country where, among the common people, the priests of Ob were so influential that if they commanded the sacrifice and the eating of an innocent babe they would be obeyed, as they had frequently been, there was no use in trying to improve things without outside, white help. These Vaudoux priests wanted to keep their dupes in the densest ignorance, and they had the power to do so, and succeeded in its use. These wretches could only be overthrown by outside influences, for even the President of the Republic was suspected of being a follower of the idolatrous craft, and no man who hoped to be elected to any important office in the land dared to speak openly against its evil practices.

These were strange facts to the boys, and long after they had retired for the night they whispered together over the wonder of it that such dense African ignorance and heathenism could exist but two days' sail from American civilization, and right in sight of almost daily travel by its very doors.

The next morning they devoted to buying some fine bananas, cocoanuts, oranges, and pineapples to send home, and to packing a box full of the most perishable things they had collected. After inspecting their bundles to see that they were all correctly marked, Ned said:—

"Doctor, you always spell the name of this country H-a-*i*-t-i, and not H-a-*y*-t-i, with a *y*, as we were taught in school. And you don't pronounce it as we do, nor did those gentlemen who called on you last night. How is that?"

"Your teachers follow the geographies, and I have never seen a geography, published in America, that does not get the names of this island all jumbled up. Some call it Hayti, and some San Domingo, but neither one is correct. Columbus named it Española, meaning 'little Spain,' and in fact, that should be the name of the whole island yet. Santo, not San, Domingo is the name he gave the city he founded, and which he named after Saint Dominic, and it is now only correctly applied to the Spanish-speaking republic of that name in the eastern half of the island. Haiti is the French attempt at spelling the original Indian name, which is supposed to have been given on account of its high mountains. To be very correct, it should be spelled H-a-ï-t-i, with a double dot over the first *i*, to show that each letter is sounded, and that the *ai* sound is not blended. The correct sound is not Hay-ti, as we spell it, but Haw-ee-tee, though here you will find many drop the sound of the *H* and shorten the word so that it sounds like Eye-tee. So hereafter, if you want to be accurate, as I know you do, you will speak of the island of Es-pan-yo'-la, the Spanish republic of Sant'-to Do-meeng'-go, and the French republic Haw-ee-tee."

In the afternoon, after four hours spent in collecting,— hours that were productive of many delightful surprises in new and beautiful species,— they returned homeward so as to be at Dave's cosy home about a half-hour before the dinner hour. Dave they found resplendent in a suit of the whitest duck, starched and ironed so stiff that it fairly cracked aloud when he walked or sat down, and Hortense was a striking picture in a blue skirt and yellow waist, with a fiery red bandanna handkerchief on her head. Even Elisha looked as though he had been scrubbed for the occasion, and the table, which had been spread outdoors under the tamarind tree, was a marvel of white linen and even whiter dishes. This was a great day for the Benton household, and they were bound to make the most of a visit from "Massa Doctah and de two young gemmen from de No'fe."

Starting with "pepper-pot," a fiery, highly-seasoned soup that the boys got well acquainted with in the following weeks, they followed with some deliciously-baked jackfish, a luscious joint of young "mountain motton," which the boys did not know was young goat until afterwards, and as fine a dish of lobster salad as one could find in a year's travel. The West Indian lobster is as different in taste as it is in shape from its northern cousin, and the boys agreed that its flavor was finer than what they were used to. With these animal foods, they were served with fried plantain, a sort of banana; "ackies," a sort of vegetable-like fruit that tasted and looked like the yolk of eggs and went well with the fish; white yams, which were much like white potatoes, mashed and baked in an oven; egg-plants; and "cho-cho," a sort of mammoth squash that the boys were satisfied to taste and let alone.

Following this substantial spread came excellent cups of coffee and some candied guavas, preserved ginger, and sliced pineapple, while a plate of fruit was placed in the centre of the table. This contained besides bananas, oranges, slices of cocoanut, and dried figs, such unknown delicacies as sapadillos, mangoes, sweet-sops, and several others of yet untried charms to the boys, who were destined to become well acquainted with and fond of them in time. As a fit ending to this sumptuous repast, to which Dave did the honors while Hortense waited on the table and kept the flies off with a mighty palm-leaf, they were introduced to a bowl of "matrimony," a delicious cooling drink compounded of lemon juice, cocoanut water, sweet-sops, claret, juice of the pineapple, and cracked ice got from a vessel then in the harbor. Such a feast as this brought from the boys almost endless praise, much to the delight of Dave and gratification of Hortense, whose skill had brought it all forth.

Not the least entertaining and surprising thing about this bountiful dinner was the sportiveness of a novel little pet that Dave was very fond and proud of. This was a tiny chameleon-like lizard, not more than six inches long and seemingly as quick as a flash of light. As soon as they sat down to the table, Harry, usually the first to observe anything unusual, called attention to a little grayish-brown lizard that was hiding in the dish of fruit on the centre of the table. Dave laughed, and giving a low whistle surprised the boys greatly by allowing the little creature, which came running to him, to disappear up his left sleeve. Then he explained that he had owned the little pet for over a year, and that from coming timidly on the table to catch flies at first, it had now grown so tame that it expected to be whistled to, and to be allowed to sit in his sleeve and occasionally run out after flies at every meal. When he chirped to it, what the boys first thought was another lizard came forth, but the Doctor explained that this was a West Indian chameleon and capable of changing its color, the bright emerald green now shown by it being generally accepted as a sign that it was contented or pleased. Dave handed it to the Doctor, who, being a stranger, was not acceptable to the changeable little reptile, and it at once began to turn to a dull ashy brown. When he gave it back to Dave, and the latter talked caressingly to it, it at once began to turn back to a vivid green.

During the meal the little pet made several sallies from its sleeve hiding-place to catch flies, but in every case it behaved very well, and refrained from getting into any of the food. But Dave explained that for a long while he had had to keep a pan of water sitting on the floor near him when at meals, and that, whenever it rushed through the butter in its chase after flies or otherwise became a nuisance, he dropped it into the water, and that in time it grew very careful about such mistakes, as it hated its duckings very much. They had had on the vessel on which he used to sail an Italian who would never take a bath until the captain commanded it; so Dave had named his tiny pet Nicodemo after that water-hating son of Italy.

CHAPTER X

AN EARTHQUAKE

Gabe — Early Morning in the Tropics — Orchids and Air-plants — Water-cocoanuts — High Prices — The Ceaseless Tom-tom — A Native Dance — The "Sablier" or Sand-box Tree — Strange Noises — Zombies, Jumbies, and Duppies — The Need of Missionaries — A Terrible Moment — Earthquakes — Cap Haitien — "The Ill-fated City." — Toussaint L'Ouverture

AFTER two days spent in further exploration of the region around Port à Paix, during which a considerable amount of material was added to the collections of insects, birds, shells, and reptiles, the party, with Dave as their guide, started along the shore on their way to the principal northern port of the island, Cap Haitien. The party numbered four human beings and four four-footed companions; for besides two horses, — on one of which some of their belongings were packed, and on the other of which they could take turns in riding, if they grew tired of walking and collecting by the way, — 'Lisha, the dog, and Gabe, a big gray mule, were of the party. The latter was the property of Dave, and on him the heaviest part of their belongings were packed. The origin of his name Dave explained as follows : —

"Dat mule? Hi! but he's a gret fellow wid his trumpet. No mattah how many mules da is wid him, he's shore to hab de las' blow on dat trumpet, so I jes' call him by de name o' dat oder las' trumpet blowah, de Angul

Gab'iel, and calls him Gabe for shote." And the boys soon found that again Dave's odd sense of humor was justified; for Gabe was a most inveterate brayer, his *ee-haws* being a feature of their trip at all hours of the day and night.

The distance from Port à Paix to Cap Haitien is but a little over thirty-five miles, but they decided to take three days to it, that they might devote most of their time to collecting in the valleys of the various streams they passed, and to one or two climbs into the foot-hills of the Plaisance Mountains, which flank the northern plain to the south and send spurs down to the very water's edge, in places. To do this it was decided that they would make a very early start, so as to do eight miles per day in the cool of the morning and four miles late in the afternoon; thus they would have the best collecting hours free and would escape the hot road during the middle of the day. Therefore they left Port à Paix just as the first streaks of gray were appearing in the east, depending on a good hot cup of cacao and a couple of bananas to nourish them sufficiently until they could enjoy the breakfast that Dave would prepare for them at the end of their morning's share of the day's trip. This is the usual custom throughout the tropics, where there is an elasticity and vigor in the early morning air that is felt at no other time in the twenty-four hours.

As the day advanced, and it became light enough to see all that was going on in the darker nooks of foliage around them, the boys discovered that they were by no means the only living beings who were availing themselves of the crisp, cool air of the dawn to be on the move. In every direction lizards of all shapes and sizes were chasing insects of even greater variety of shape and size, in pursuit of their early breakfast. On every hand birds were doing much the same thing, and those of their kind who were in search of honey and other sweets, the humming birds in particular, were especially active in their rush from flower to flower. Nor was the animal life all that gave proof of a vigorous awakening with the returning morning; the air was laden — in places almost too heavily laden — with the perfume of flowers that by midday would be wilted and unable to give the passer-by any idea of the loveliness that had been theirs while they were yet bathed in dew. Among these, the flowers of certain orchids were especially noticeable, and, when they camped for the day in a shady nook by the side of a small stream that came rushing out of the hills, Harry was so impressed by this that he said:—

"Doctor, how do these orchids and other air-plants get enough nourishment, the way they grow, to make such an amount of smell? Do their roots run into the trees they grow on, so deep as to gain strength from them?"

"The further you go into the tropics," was the Doctor's reply, "the more you will be impressed with the importance of air-plants in the vegetable world. Every big tree here is an aërial botanical garden. Giant plants perched in the fork of a forest monarch will send their roots to the ground, and it is these cords and ropes that are so useful in scores of ways to the natives of such countries. Others send their *lianas* or vegetable ropes, trailing from tree to tree in massive festoons, until they resemble the rigging of some ship after a storm. Frequently you will meet a tree covered with gorgeous flowers, and on going to the other side of it, will discover that, while it is there as densely covered, it is with totally different flowers. On examination it will be found that none of these owe their origin to the tree, or extract their nourishment from it, but that all are the product of air-plants that send their roots to the earth and only depend on the tree for support, or that appear to get from the air alone all the nourishment they need. Climbing ferns, vanillas, orchids of hundreds of kinds, and a thousand other vegetable parasites of the same sort live in this way; I have myself counted twenty-seven different forms of plant life thus growing, without counting the many forms of mosses, lichens, and other minor growths that covered one tree.

"One group of air-plants, the roots of which do not extend to the ground, and the presence of which on a tree does not in the least appear to weaken it, seem to get their nourishment principally by their broad, sheath-like leaves, which form cups around the main stalk and hold rain water for a long time. This must be of great value to the plant during the dry season, and the fact that many insects are attracted to and drowned in these tiny wells would seem to account for one source of the plant's nourishment, as the insects rapidly decay under such conditions."

With Dave, Harry went to a cabin near camp, and for a few pennies bought as many "water-cocoanuts" as they could use for the day. The ripened cocoanut, as they had known it in the North, the boys had already learned was a very inferior, insipid thing compared with the delicate, luscious, partly ripe nut, known in that stage as the water-cocoanut, on account of the always cool and nourishing fluid, the "milk," which it contained. After drinking this fluid from two nuts and then scooping out the delicious, jelly-like pulp, which had not yet begun to harden into the indigestible mass that is found in the fully ripe nut, it occurred to Ned that his share of the treat had not cost as much as a small glass of soda water at home, and he remarked: —

"Travelling is pretty cheap here, isn't it? One can travel for a few cents if he knows how and is content with Creole ways; can't he, Doctor?"

"Yes, usually. But that depends on when you come here and what you have to offer in exchange. American or English gold goes a great way here; but if you happened along this way during one of their many rebellions with only Haitian paper money in your pocket, you would not fare so well. A historian tells of a time here, not so very long ago, when one dollar in American gold would buy $400 in Haitian paper money, and a guide asked $2000, in that money, for three days' service, and a claret lemonade cost $30. And that happened right along this north shore."

That night, although the dense foliage around them had prevented their being aware of it by sight, their ears informed them that they had camped near a settlement; for no sooner had it grown dark and the natives had time for their evening meal than there began not very far away the monotonous beating of the tom-tom or native drum. At first the boys, who had once or twice during their trip heard the noise at a distance, did not understand it; but the Doctor explained that by stretching a dried goat or pig skin head over a butter tub, a large section of bamboo, a bucket, or even a tin oil-can with the top cut off, the natives made a rude sort of drum, from the incessant beating of which they appeared to derive much pleasure.

The tom-tom has a rather pleasing, soothing sound at a distance, and harmonizes well with the endless din of insects and other creeping things in a tropical night, so as to lull one to sleep in a very delightful manner. But for comfort's sake it should be at least half a mile away; and he is an unhappy wretch who has a tom-tom player for a near neighbor and is compelled night after night, and perhaps often all night, to listen to the maddening monotony of its thump, thump, thump.

"What fun can they get out of that everlasting bang, banging?" Ned asked.

"They will tell you, if you ask them," replied the Doctor, "that that is the way they were taught; and their great-grandparents would have told you, in their day, that so it was done in Africa. Of course their principal use for the tom-tom is as an accompaniment to the music of the dance, and I imagine that is what is going on over there. If you care to, while I am fixing our things to go out after moths to-night, Dave can take you over there, where you can get a peep at their dancing. It is an odd sight, and one well worth seeing. But you must be careful not to appear to be laughing at them, if they notice you looking on."

When, under Dave's guidance, the boys reached the

neighborhood of the sound, they found that not only two tom-toms, but a rude violin and two bamboo flutes also, lent their music to the occasion, each performer disdaining anything like time or harmony, and each indulging in a sort of musical go-as-you-please. In this they were followed by the dancers, for it was impossible to detect any regular figure or rule of procedure; each couple, and often each individual, appeared to follow their own ideas of what would be most startling. Posturing, contorting, hoe-downs, double shuffles, walk-arounds, jigs, flings, polkas, waltzes, and even the orderly minuet or reel seemed to be mixed in one hopeless tangle of humanity; and the boys came away, after a half-hour of silent, intent watching, much mystified and much amused.

"Why, Doctor," said Harry, "that music, I suppose they call it, kept on steadily all the time, without any change in tune or in the form of dance; and it is going yet!"

"So it will be when we come back from our collecting, I think you will find," the Doctor replied. And he was right. Two and one-half hours after, on their homeward way they stopped for a moment, and the players were playing as ever, the figure of the dance was the same muddle as before, and, apparently, the same dancers were still on the floor, or rather the sod. And so it was long after midnight, Dave told them the next morning, as he heard when he was up to replenish their camp fire.

Very early the next morning, before daylight or it was time to get up, they were all awakened by a succession of small explosions, much like the repeated firings of a pistol, but not so loud and very near at hand. Both boys were up in an instant, and were not a little nervous, as the many tales of Haitian history they had already heard came flocking to their memories. One word from Dave, in his hammock outside the tent, set the Doctor to laughing and caused him to say:—

"Sure enough! The 'sablier,' as they call it, or the sand-box tree, *Hura crepitans*. The noise is caused by the bursting of the large eight-sided pods of a tree near by, which, owing to their being ripe, pop open with this pistol-like sound and scatter their seed around. I remember on my first trip to the West Indies, years ago, that a mischievous friend nearly frightened me out of a year's growth by putting four or five pods in my bureau, and one after another they went off with an appalling report, made much louder in the dead of night by being in a bureau drawer and in a small room."

"It seems to me there are a great many strange noises in this country, anyhow," said Ned. "I woke up last night, and while I was listening to the thousands of voices of insects that with the lizards and tree-toads made altogether a mighty roar, I heard a very peculiar mumbling sound that seemed to me to come from the hills above us, yet the ground trembled slightly, I thought. What was it, do you think, Doctor?"

"Probably what geologists call subsidence of some great land mass in the caves beneath us. Nearly all of this island is underlaid with a network of caverns, and the continual dripping of the water in them at times detaches masses of earth that in falling send up a dull sound and very naturally shake the vicinity slightly. Some of these are small and very local, but some must be very large, for their effects are heard or felt for many miles. These are dignified by being classed among earthquakes, and no doubt account for most of the minor shocks felt here in recent years."

"The one I heard last night was quite loud, and certainly made me feel very uncomfortable," said Ned.

"Yes, unless one understands them they sound very uncanny, and it is no wonder that the natives believe them to be caused by Zombies, as they call them."

"What are Zombies?" asked Harry.

"Zombies, as the French negroes call them, or Jumbies, as they are in English, are the spirits of departed ones who have lived evil and spiteful lives here and who redouble their energy in doing harm in the spirit life. They also include many of the assistants of the Evil One, sent here to work mischief among the living. Duppies, which you have heard them allude to by calling butterflies 'duppy-bats,' are the fairies, brownies, wood-nymphs, and other harmless spirits, rather inclined to good, kindly acts. But the Zombies are seriously feared and certain places, such as certain caves or trees, that are believed to be frequented by them at night, are never ventured near, if by any possibility it can be avoided. Half the ills they are heir to, from a thorn in the foot to a dead wife or mother, or a burned house or an earthquake-shaken village, they attribute to the Zombies, and it is largely to curry favor with the great master of the Zombies, the All-powerfull Snake, and get him to remove the effects of the persecution, that they so constantly sacrifice to snakes and pay so much of their slender incomes to the priests of this witchcraft, the *papaloi*, whose dupes they are."

"Dat's de fac', and no mistake," said Dave who had been listening. "If dey had de Meffodises, Baptisses, and Prisbyte'yuns all a'fighten togedder fo' day souls, dey wouldn't hab no time nor no notion fo' all sech debilment as Zombies, and dat's what I tell them ebery day. What day want is de 'lightenment what we'se got in de No'fe."

The Doctor made no reply, but he smiled and shook his head in approval to the boys, to signify that, in his rough way, Dave had hit the nail on the head, as he usually did.

A day of great activity in the collecting field — for the boys now found themselves in the very thick of a most entrancing and exceedingly rich region for their work — and an evening of equal success at the sugared trees, resulted in sending two thoroughly tired boys to bed somewhat earlier than usual. So tired were they that both prophesied that they would not once stir during the night, little realizing how sleepless part of it was to prove.

They had not been in bed long enough for the Doctor to have finished his usual methodical work of putting everything to rights before retiring, although both had already fallen asleep, when they were suddenly awakened by a sensation the like of which was entirely new to them. Afterwards Harry said he started up from dreaming that he was on the sea in a violent storm; but Ned, who could recall no dream, woke imagining that the tent was being pounded to pieces over them. 'Lisha was howling in a most dismal fashion, Dave was heard speaking reassuringly to the horses, which the boys saw by the light he was turning loose from the trees where they were tied, and Gabe was uttering the most terrific brays imaginable.

The usual overpowering roar of the night life in the forests was hushed into a solemn stillness that was most impressive, almost terrible; and although then they could not explain it, both boys said, afterwards, that they had a distinct feeling that something fearful was going to happen. Just as Ned was about to voice their wonder at it all to the Doctor, who was helping Dave with the horses, the question was answered for them and their fears increased an hundred-fold by the sudden motion of the ground under their feet, first to this side, then to that, and then with a sudden motion, apparently downwards. A bucket two-thirds full of water just outside the tent, Ned remembered afterwards, was so shaken that some of its contents was spilled, and the bull's-eye lantern which always burned dimly at the door of the tent was swaying to and fro like the pendulum of a clock. As suddenly as it had begun, the motion stopped, and both boys sank down to the ground, sick with fear, nauseated as in seasickness with the rocking of the earth, and in a cold perspiration. Seeing that they were awake and about, the Doctor hurried to them with these assuring words:—

"Don't be alarmed, boys! We are in perfect safety, I assure you! This sort of earthquake never causes fissures or earthcracks, and we are not in a building which can topple on our heads and crush us to death, which is the only serious danger from this sort of shake."

These were comforting words to the boys, who knew the

Doctor too well to feel any doubt of his words under such circumstances; but notwithstanding their returning confidence, each recurring motion of the earth, of which there were nine in the following three hours, made them feel far from comfortable. It was a strange sensation to them, who had always looked upon the earth's surface as a stable place on which was safety, to find it rocking and trembling with a sea-like motion, and to be told that in reality the sea was a safer surface in earthquake times. But their fear finally wore away, and the boys found themselves regarding each shock with less dread.

"Earthquakes are one of the things you can't learn about by reading, evidently," said Ned. "I thought I had a good idea of what it was like, but I find my reading had given me but a faint idea of how really frightful the sensation is when one wakes up to find the ground cutting up such capers. Does a person ever get used to them so as no longer to fear them, Doctor?"

"You will find many persons, especially among the Spanish half-breeds, who are inclined to be a very boastful people, who will assure you that they have no fear of such things and do not allow them to interfere with their usual occupations. But they are either foolishly bragging, or else they have never felt a really severe shock. I have met such people in quantities, and when the time came for the test I have always observed them to be the first to scuttle off to an open place of comparative safety, quite oblivious to their duty to help the aged or less active. However brave one may be, or however long he may have lived in an earthquake country, there is that in a really serious shock or succession of shocks that will unnerve the bravest and make cowards of those least susceptible to ordinary fear. I have seen the ground rocking so that tall cocoanut palms were bent almost to the ground, the surface of the earth undulated like the waves in the sea, and massive stone buildings came toppling down like the toy houses we used to make of blocks; and at such times I have always felt terrified beyond expression, and every one around me acted or looked the same."

On the evening of the next day they arrived in the little city of Cap Haitien, once an important port of 75,000 prosperous inhabitants, now a town of hardly 11,000 souls, many of whom live in the utmost squalor and degradation. Along their route that day, they saw a few signs that the earthquake of the night before had shaken down some dead tree limbs, and one or two houses had suffered slightly; but as the buildings they passed were, for the most part, the ordinary bamboo huts with palm-leaf thatches, there was but little sign of serious damage to be expected. In Cap Haitien, they found, on inquiring at the principal boarding-place, where they went at once, that there had been but three shocks felt, and each of those but slight, so that there was no damage reported there.

As the boys started out to see what sugaring for moths would produce on the outskirts of the town, that night, the Doctor told them that for many years Cap Haitien had been known to historians as "the ill-fated City," and, at their request he told them some stories from its history, in explanation of that name.

The town had been first settled as the site for a

European colony in 1670, soon after the French buccaneers had possessed themselves of their part of the island from the Spanish conquerors. The French were quick to see that this was the best harbor and pleasantest place on the north shore, which was and still is very superior to the south, both in climate and fertility. But from the first, and always, the French showed that their fiery tempers made poor slave-owners of them, and in 1791, at the very height of its prosperity and power, when it claimed to be the chief port in the West Indies, on the night of August 22d, the slaves on the plantations in the interior plains, most of whose masters had their homes in the wealthy little city, rose in a body at a preconcerted signal; and before any one was aware of their intention, every estate had been put to the torch. Cane fields burn like tinder, and the addition of storehouses of rum, and sugar mills, soon lit up the whole heavens with a vast conflagration. All the pent-up hatred of long years, on the part of the slaves for their cruel masters, burst forth, and they rushed upon the defenceless planters and their families, butchering them by the hundred, and throwing their dismembered bodies into the flames.

For two years, bloody skirmishes were kept up by the whites of the town and the blacks who had taken possession of the plantations, when France sent three commissioners and a fleet of naval vessels to quell the uprising. Tiring of inactivity and angered by the arrogance of the free mulattoes, the sailors of the fleet entered the town on the 20th of June, 1793, intent on humbling the inhabitants. Many whites took sides with the sailors, and under the very eyes of the blacks in the plains the opposing sides began to attack each other in the town. Finding the two sides evenly balanced, the commissioners called to their aid the blacks, and these were brought in from the surrounding country and with those liberated from the jails were armed; then this savage and blood-thirsty horde were turned loose on the miserable townspeople with unlimited power to kill and maim and burn to their ignorant hearts' content. The negroes, caring not whom they attacked, so long as it was the French, poured into the ill-fated town like a river of fire. Hundreds of the towns-people were drowned in the attempt to escape to the vessels in the harbor, hundreds perished by the sword or by fire. The flames were applied to large quantities of oils and pitch in the storehouses, and soon the town looked like a volcano with a mighty column of fire and dense smoke above it. The governor, seeing the disastrous results of the foolhardy experiment of arming the blacks, sailed from the harbor to Norfolk, Virginia, with over 10,000 exiles, most of whom settled in the United States.

Pestilence followed close on this disaster, and those who were spared by the fever continued the bloody feuds between the blacks on one hand and the whites and mulattoes on the other. Then Spain, owning the eastern end of the island, undertook to control the blacks, and the latter united with the French against English, Spanish, and mulatto forces. This alliance with their old enemies, the French, was mainly brought about by a leader of the blacks known as Toussaint L'Ouverture, who for fifty-two years had been a plantation slave, and, as many believe, a priest of witchcraft, who, in return for his influence over the blacks, was made Lieutenant-Governor of Haiti by the French. Having shown remarkable energy and unusual intelligence, considering his color and former condition, the French government appointed him to a military position bearing the high-sounding title of General-in-Chief of Santo Domingo; and in the proud city, where but six years before a black dared not to speak his mind aloud, one of the down-trodden race now lived in state, lord over the highest of his former masters.

France soon tired of the idea of a black vested with such great powers in what was once her proudest and most valued colony, and she sent a French general to replace him. Toussaint willingly retired to a neighboring plantation, which had come into his possession; but his followers would not remain quiet without their leader, and they suddenly assembled in the plain again by night, intent on burning the city, now largely rebuilt. Suddenly Toussaint appeared among them, and only his presence restrained them from again killing the French, who were allowed to embark for France.

By 1802 prosperity had in a great measure returned to the city, so great is the fertility of the surrounding country, and so ready were the black generals to use their authority to work the estates they had seized, with the labor of their soldiers. Then Napoleon determined to humble the rich and rebellious colony. At first he sent 25,000 troops against about as many blacks, and these numbers were afterwards considerably increased. The blacks were commanded by Toussaint, with Generals Dessalines and

Christophe as his aids. The former had been a plantation slave, and the latter a waiter in a café. Both died kings, though neither of them could read when first called to power. When the French fleet appeared, the town was cleared of all its population save the armed men, and at the first firing from the ships the houses were systematically fired. Again Cap Haitien went up in flame, and on the next morning there was nothing but blackened ruins where the French had intended to make their headquarters in a handsome city: $20,000,000, is estimated to have been the loss. The French immediately began rebuilding the town, but the yellow fever brought their enterprise to a stop, and before it was through with them, out of 34,000 soldiers, 24,000 were dead, 7,000 were invalided, and but 3,000 remained for active service, in nine months. For a month longer they held out, and then surrendered to General Dessalines, the former plantation black.

From this date until 1811 the city enjoyed comparative rest, only marred by the massacre of all the French by order of Dessalines, who had been declared king. He, having been put to death, probably by his own followers jealous of his power, was followed by the café waiter, Christophe, who established an hereditary black monarchy, the first and only one of its kind outside of Africa, having himself crowned Henry I., and instituting a nobility with such ridiculous titles as the Duke of Lemonade, the Duke of Marmalade, and others equally grotesque. After a barbarous reign he died by his own hand in his castle of Sans Souci in the environs of the city, Oct. 8, 1820. His rival, President Boyer of the South of Haiti, assumed the reins of government, and for twenty-two years the city knew a season of quiet unprecedented in rebellious Haiti. Then, on the 7th of May, 1842, without any warning, the whole north shore of the island was convulsed by a terrific earthquake, and Cap Haitien was again left a shapeless mass of crumbled ruins. Whole towns were crushed, thousands were killed, and to this day the older people in the towns tell how the country people rushed in to plunder the ruins and were too eager for ill-gotten booty to lend a helping hand to their dying and maimed countrymen. Even the soldiers from the neighboring barracks aided in plundering the stores that were filled with goods, instead of lending their aid to their friends and even to their relatives in their sore distress. From this last blow Cap Haitien has never recovered and shows no signs of recovering; and in their inhuman actions those who were saved from the earthquake to join in the pilfering and looting set forth more plainly than could volumes of print the true Haitian character.

CHAPTER XI

INTO THE WILDERNESS

The Palace of Sans Souci — The Citadel of La Terriere — Productiveness of the Land — Along the Coast — A Squalid Land — Port au Prince — A Paris of Mud — A Useful Lesson — The American Minister — President Hippolyte — A Strong Contrast — Start of the Cavalcade — A Funeral Procession — Vaudoux Orgies — Snake Worship

THE next day was principally given up to an examination of the ruins of the Palace of Sans Souci, built by Christophe when he was reigning as Henry I., and of the Citadel of La Terriere. Coming out to these from the squalor of the present town, with the refuse in its undrained streets putrefying in the hot sun and its irregular rows of miserable hovels in which dwelt the most debased specimens of humanity the boys had ever seen, it was hard to imagine that the time had once been when this region was one of the proudest and wealthiest of the Western World. But that it had been so, the signs of the stately beauty of the vine-overgrown palace and the massive walls of the fortification amply attested. Nothing but a wealthy community could have built such piles as these; and the ruins of the citadel, standing aloft on a mountain summit nearly 3000 feet high, with its walls yet 80 feet high in some places and 16 feet thick, with many of the formidable guns, abandoned nearly a century ago, still in place, were a silent reproach to the miserable people in the valley below, who were allowing themselves as they had allowed it to lapse back into uselessness.

"Doctor," said Harry, "this land must have had lots of people in those days and they must have produced more on their land to afford such magnificence as all this, must they not?"

"Certainly they must. At the close of the last century it is known that there were 612,000 inhabitants in Haiti, of whom 46,000 were whites, and, although by this time they should have increased quite fourfold, by all laws of population, such is the effect of their incessant warfare and wicked habits of life that they have added but little to their numbers, and all the whites have gone. In the middle of the last century the sugar plantations of this island controlled the markets of the world, as they might still; to-day they get much of their sugar from foreign countries. In 1789 a half million laborers cultivated 793 sugar plantations, 3117 coffee estates, 3150 indigo plantations, and 735 cotton plantations; to-day more than that number of laborers work nothing but a few paltry coffee estates, where the methods pursued are so careless that Haitian coffee is of the lowest grades. Under Toussaint l'Ouverture, 470,000 people produced about $25,000,000 worth of coffee, sugar, cotton, cacao, indigo, etc., for export; while but 30 years later, under Boyer, 715,000 people produced less than $8,500,000 worth, and the showing has been growing gradually poorer each decade."

In many other ways and with many other facts and figures the Doctor impressed upon the boys the sure and steady decay of the Haitian people, under entire and untrammelled black rule, that they might be all the more impressed with the contrast that awaited them under a mixed government in Jamaica.

After a few days spent in collecting in and around Cap Haitien, with one day given up to a short excursion into the rugged interior, the Doctor found a coasting vessel about to make the trip to Port au Prince, touching at the principal ports on the way. As this would afford the boys an excellent opportunity to see something more of Haitian town life, give them time to sort and arrange their collection, which had been accumulating very rapidly of late, and also be a good chance to use a deep-sea dredge and trawl, in an attempt to add to their knowledge of marine forms, he decided to ship on this vessel, as there were to be but few passengers and they could have plenty of room to themselves.

This trip was made in a thoroughly leisurely and characteristically tropical way; at every port they made, the Doctor and his young companions had ample opportunity to go ashore and inspect the locality, so slow was the work of unloading and loading. This also made it possible for them to send Dave back to Port à Paix with the horses they had hired and then overland with 'Lisha and Gabe to meet them at Port au Prince.

There was a monotonously squalid similarity about the towns at which they touched, which left a general impression of the degraded poverty of the whole country, and there was but little at each place worthy of special observation. They were naturally interested in their first harbor beyond Port à Paix, St. Nicholas Môle, because it was the first harbor in the island into which Columbus sailed on his way east from Cuba, and because for some years the United States has been trying to gain possession of that harbor by special treaty, so that it may establish there a coaling and supply station for its navy in West Indian waters. The harbor, landlocked and with deep water throughout, runs in eastwardly for about a mile and then bends northward almost at right angles for about three-fourths of a mile further, while its mouth, with Cape Môle on one hand and Cape St. Nicholas on the other about three-fourths of a mile apart, is so formed as to render its defence very easy.

At Port à Piment, so named because it was once a principal port for the shipment of *pimento*, or West Indian allspice, the boys found a mere village backed by a range of rather barren hills, while at Gonaives, at the extreme northeastern corner of the great bay of that name, they found a town of perhaps 6000 inhabitants, on the upper arm of an inlet affording an excellent harbor. St. Marc was their only other port before reaching Port au Prince, and it they found to be an uninteresting town of about 3000 souls with nothing but its coffee trade to attract passing notice.

These five ports, although the distance between no two of them was over a few hours' run, took as many days, but the time was well spent in sight-seeing on land or in classifying collections and occasionally examining the dredge that was allowed to drag behind the vessel part of the time. This raised a number of sea forms, of both animal and plant life, that were curious and new to the boys, which the Doctor told them were worth saving as additions to their collections.

Port au Prince, the capital city of Haiti, the Doctor told them was variously estimated to contain from twenty to thirty thousand inhabitants. It is the show city of the island, most of the inhabitants firmly believing that it quite equals any of the proud capitals of Europe or America. As they sailed into the harbor, which is an open bay too shallow to allow of vessels of any size coming near the wharves, they noticed that it stood low in a swampy plain, with the main range of mountains some miles in the interior, and that there appeared to be no tides in the harbor to take away the filth of the city's drainage and bear away the insufferable stench of the water thus made impure. Yet, while they were observing these things, a score or more of boats put out from the shore with several colored boys in each, and they were soon made aware of the fact that, notwithstanding the foul condition of the water, the new arrivals had come out in the hope that some of the passengers would throw silver pieces overboard, after which the darkies would jump into this horrid mess and capture them.

The Doctor, in describing to them the form of the town, and purposely saying nothing of its condition, had mentioned streets with high-sounding names, Le Grand Rue being among the number, and the boys were quite unprepared to find these streets little better than gutters winding their way through hog-wallows. Yet as they landed on a tumble-down wharf and carefully picked their way from stone to stone through the filthy streets, the odor of which beggared description, and noticed the irregularly placed wooden houses, many of them but little better than mere hovels, they realized how little real basis there was for the grandiloquent and boastful claims which the Haitians made for their city.

The boys were glad when Dave joined them the second day of their stay in Port au Prince and the Doctor told them that there was nothing to prevent them from at once setting to work to prepare for their trip into the interior. The ridiculous attempt at show made by the wealthier negroes of the city was disgusting to them, reminding them, as Harry put it, of a lot of monkeys in fine clothes. The sight of a few hundred ragged, barefooted soldiers, no two holding their guns alike, and all of them marching in the most helter-skelter fashion, with more than a dozen "Generals," wobbling about on their miserable little horses, was such a parody on a real army, that Ned expressed the opinion that he would like to come down to the island with about fifty New York policemen, picked from "the Broadway squad," and run these wretched black mimics of real soldiers into the sea.

For these opinions they got a lecture from the Doctor. He reminded them that they, the descendants of Anglo-Saxons who had never been enslaved, had for many centuries known what it was to enjoy their rights, while these Africans, as he had before told them, were but a few years out of the most degrading bondage imaginable, in which their ancestors had lived for at least 5000 years, as shown by the pictures and inscriptions on the most ancient Egyptian monuments. When they got to Jamaica and when they visited other West Indian islands, they would see that the blacks had been making astonishing progress in civilization and culture. Then they would understand that these wretched Haitians were not to be despised because they were negroes, but were to be pitied because they had made the mistake of attempting self-civilization away from the influence of the whites. Haiti and Santo Domingo are, even to-day, the richest and most fertile spots in all the Americas; every useful thing can be grown in them, and most minerals are believed to be hidden in their mountains in very considerable quantities. Were these bounteous regions to be opened freely to Anglo-Saxon enterprise, in a few decades no land on the earth would be able to surpass them for wealth and charm. But under the present rule, it could not be denied, they were certainly becoming less civilized and more degraded every year.

"People who claim that all men are born equal ought to come down here and take a look around," said Ned.

"I think you, in common with many others, misunderstand that theory, or fact, as it really is," the Doctor replied. "No sane man can claim to believe that all are born equal, as a comparison in our own color will easily show. Surely, the idiotic children of some wretched drunken father and mother, who have, from the first, had to be kept in a public insane asylum, cannot have been born equal with a Shakespeare, a Lincoln, a Napoleon, or a Bismarck. What is meant by the expression is, that all men, however humble or obscure their origin, however feeble or criminal their minds, are born with equal rights. Whether they get those rights is not in the question; that they are entitled to them alike, without any consideration of their position in life, all honorable men must admit."

It was decided that before they left the town, it was both their duty and privilege to call upon President Hippolyte at the presidential palace. The Doctor had letters of introduction to the American Minister, Mr. John Durham, of Philadelphia, a young, fine looking, very light mulatto gentleman, who was well educated, and was altogether a very pleasant man to know, and in his company they called by appointment on the President. The formality and pomp that were observed, prepared the boys to meet a very impressive and commanding personage, and when they were at last ushered into the presence of a black man with nothing but his clothes to indicate that there was any difference between him and his fellow countrymen, it was with great difficulty that their surprise was kept from showing itself in their faces. After the usual formal words of greeting and assurances of respect had been exchanged on both sides and the purpose of their proposed visit into the interior had been explained to Mr. Hippolyte, he informed them that he would see that they were provided with suitable letters of introduction that would secure them a safe and pleasant trip inland. Then with a few more words of mere formality, they withdrew. Having bidden Minister Durham good-bye, after accepting an invitation to take dinner with him that evening, they returned to their hotel, where they were soon busy in the midst of packing a lot of their collections to ship on the next northbound steamer. While they were thus engaged, the Doctor said,

"We have just had an excellent example of the differences that can exist in the negro races, just as they can in our own. Mr. Durham is a product of Northern civilization and freedom as it is to be observed in Philadelphia, where the colored man is given a better opportunity to develop his mind and make headway in the world than anywhere else in our country; while President Hippolyte is a natural product of Haitian ignorance and lack of progressiveness."

The Doctor had planned the trip to last about three weeks, so that they would proceed directly into the interior, cross the Santo Domingan frontier in the southeast, encamp a few days on the shores of Laguna Enriquillo, then proceed to ascend the La Selle range of mountains, attempting to climb the main peak of La Selle, and from there proceed along the southern coast to Jacmel, where they could either take the Royal Mail Line direct to Jamaica, or could take a coasting-vessel back to Port au Prince, and from there proceed to Jamaica by the Atlas Line. To carry this out, they found it would be necessary to make the journey with four horses besides the mule, Gabe; so Dave found an intelligent, trustworthy black man who had made much the same trip as the guide of a Boston collector of birds, a few years before, and he also hired the necessary horses. Heretofore, as the Doctor told them, they had had experience with only the easiest and pleasantest forms of camp life; now they were to try their talents in battling with the interior wilderness and if they could come out of that none the worse for the wear, he would know that they were of the true stuff that explorers were made of, and that it was safe to take them anywhere.

The first few days did not differ materially from what they had already become acquainted with, save that they had left the sea and the plains behind and had come into such interminable ranges of mountains that there hardly seemed to be a square foot of level ground anywhere. Whites had disappeared and even mulattoes were scarce, but as they had come prepared to depend on their own cooking entirely, they were none the worse for that. On the night of their fourth day, after much tedious mountain climbing up and down bridle paths, that were simply the nearly dry beds of mountain torrents, and an evening given up to the active pursuit of some very rare moths, they were just about to retire when in the distance they heard a most indescribable din, that was clearly made by human voices mingled with the beloved tom-toms and bamboo fifes and that was evidently rapidly coming their way.

"Dem horses bettah be tied good an' strong," said Dave, on hearing it. "Day's city horses an' day is boun' to brek loose when dat dere 'cession comes 'long." With which remark he and his assistant Henri busied themselves with visiting the five trees where their charges were tied and making sure that they were well secured.

"A procession, does he call it?" asked Ned. "What sort of a procession is it; do they have political parades out here in the back woods?"

"Well, hardly," the Doctor replied, laughing at the idea. "It is most likely to be a funeral procession."

"A funeral! Well that rather goes ahead of anything ridiculous we have yet heard of them. Do they bury their dead at night, and do they make a jollification of it?" Ned asked, as he heard the laughter and shouts that were mingled with the unearthly din.

In a few minutes the procession of perhaps seventy-five men, women, and children was abreast of them, and there was no trouble in discovering that it was, as the Doctor had imagined, a funeral procession; for after the half dozen tom-tom and fife players came four men carrying a coffin on two poles over their shoulders. But even that was not by any means all the proof of the solemn nature of the reason for their being out at such a late hour; for on the shoulders of four other men was carried an ordinary chair, and in that, tied fast in a sitting position, was carried along the corpse of an elderly woman, nodding and bobbing around in a most gruesome and uncanny fashion. This sight sent a cold chill through the boys, who had always been taught to regard the dead with a sort of veneration almost akin to fear. And after the howling, hooting mob had disappeared around a turn in the path, they sat and looked at each other and at the Doctor speechless with wonder. Finally Ned got his voice and asked the Doctor whether that was an ordinary burial ceremony, or whether it was not some very unusual performance.

"What you have just seen," was the reply, "illustrates how deeply rooted the old superstitions and habits of their native Africa have remained in these poor heathen in spite of the century or two of Christian teaching they have had since coming here. No doubt the Catholic priest, if there is one living near here, has already performed the rites of his church at the home of the dead. But after he has been dismissed, the relatives have called in the Papaloi, or priest of the snake worship, and to his ceremonies they will give more heed and attach more importance, as well as pay much more for them, than to those of the Christian father. After the latter left the house they, probably, held a sort of walk-around, — the dead being placed in the middle of the room, — howling and wailing, singing and roaring, together with eating and drinking, being the principal forms of the ceremony there. The next ceremony you have just seen, and the last, which will probably be enacted near here, will be at the grave's side, and will be even worse and less decorous than the others."

"This snake worship or Vaudoux seems to be mixed up in everything they do," said Harry.

"The worship of the snake, you know, is as old a form of idolatry as any of which we have historic knowledge, dating back even farther than sun worship. It is so grounded in the negro character that they hardly dare move or think without considering it, where they still observe it. While it can be found in greatly modified forms wherever the blacks live, even New York and Philadelphia having a few Vaudoux priests, without doubt, and there called 'voodoo doctors,' still the interior of Haiti must be admitted to be its headquarters in America. So thoroughly does it enter into daily life here, that no funeral, wedding, birth, or even christening is considered complete without its Vaudoux ceremonials."

"Why can't we go and see what they are doing at the grave, Doctor?" Ned asked.

"I hardly think it is entirely safe," was the reply. "Should they see us spying upon them, it would probably end in trouble; might even end very seriously, in fact. There are a good many ways in which they could seriously annoy us or make our expedition impossible. They might even go to the lengths of injuring our horses in some way, or they might poison our drinking-water, so as to make us all sick for a week or two, even if we escaped with our lives. It is rather too risky an experiment to try, don't you think so?" The Doctor addressed his last remarks to Dave, who came up at that moment, knowing that Henri could not understand English and that Dave was entirely free from any taint of the Vaudoux superstition.

"Tell yo' what I ken do, Massah Doctor," Dave said; "I ken tek de young gen'men wid me, and mek believe we is gone after some mo' o' dem night-butterflies. Den you ken keep Henri yere an' I reckon we ken find de bur'yal-place in de dark. I'll be mighty careful o' Massah Ned and Massah Harry, an' yo' needn' hab no uneasiness about dem."

"Well, boys, if you are willing to risk it, under such good guidance, I guess you can go. I'll trust Dave to get you out all right with a first-class excuse, if you are detected; but you must obey him in every particular, for there is no hiding the fact that it is ticklish business, at the best, this peeping around after the Vaudoux practices."

Each of the three having put his pistol belt on and Dave having tied up 'Lisha, so that he would not follow them and disclose their presence by shaking to death any Haitian dog that might come sniffling around them, they started off, Dave in the lead down the rocky path, occasionally flashing the bull's-eye lantern on the worst parts, although keeping it most of the time perfectly dark. After about an eighth of a mile of the most difficult scrambling, harder work than would have been five miles of mountain climbing by daylight, they came suddenly on an opening in the undergrowth, which was enclosed in a cactus hedge and in the centre of which stood a bamboo hut, back of which burned a fire of considerable size. This clearing or yard was well filled with the funeral party, and on a rude bier was the coffin in which was the corpse, although the lid had not yet been put in place.

Dave whispered to the boys to follow him with great care and utter no sound under any circumstances; then he led them to a point where a break in the cactus hedge made it easy for them to see all that was going on in the yard without running much risk of being seen. Near the coffin stood a tall, commanding man, as black as coal but with almost snow-white hair on his uncovered head, who the boys knew instinctively was the priest of the witchcraft. He was swaying from side to side in front of a box that seemed to have a wicker-work front, and into this he was constantly sticking the fingers of his right hand. After watching him closely for a time, they saw that as the crowd, which was formed in a huge ring that was slowly dancing round him, passed him the leaders pressed their hands in his and immediately his sought the box. Still closer watching disclosed the fact that offerings of small coins appeared to be changing from the possession of the crowd in the ring into the box, through the hands of the Papaloi.

Rapidly the dancing ring grew wilder and wilder, and the boys noticed that near the fire there was a large pot which most of them, even the younger ones, frequently visited for a drink, and the whiffs of odor that came from it told that it was some intoxicant that thus attracted them. After a while the younger people and the more feeble of the old ones began to drop away from the whirling mob, and one by one the stronger and more active began to grow more wildly excited, bowing and assuming strange postures before first the coffin and then the box. Then the fire was nearly put out and the robust dancers now left began to tear off their clothing and to grow actually frantic in their savagery. Through it all the Papaloi kept up the same monotonous swaying to and fro, the same monotonous passing of his hand from the circling line of dancers to the box, and never for a moment flagged in a sing-song sort of incantation over the dead body.

As the crowd continued to grow even more frantic and the din was such that they could speak to each other with safety, Dave called the boys' attention to the fact that there was something to be seen dimly moving in the box, and told them that was the snake to which the blacks were making their offerings of coin and promises of fruit and vegetables to be delivered at the hut of its priest, the Papaloi, on the morrow, sagely adding,

"It'll be mighty lil' money or gahden truck dat de snake 'll get, after dat ole debil, de Voodoo man, gets what he teks out as his share, sho' 'nough."

Then as he told them this performance might continue until almost daylight, they turned and followed him back to the tent, which they reached well worn out, but glad that they had had an opportunity to see what, probably, no other American boys had ever seen under like unusual and dangerous circumstances.

"Yer we is, Massah Doctor; and no one de wiser ob ouah bein' neah de debilment. It war jes' de same ole snake-dance what yo' an' I'se seen befo'," said Dave, as they rejoined the Doctor.

"Well, boys, what do you think of a Vaudoux burial?" the Doctor asked. "It's hardly as solemn a ceremony as we are accustomed to, is it?"

"I should say not!" exclaimed Ned. "I must confess I don't see what it is all about. Why they do all the howling and dancing, and why they pay that gray-haired old impostor all the money they can scrape together, is too much for me."

"Simply because they firmly believe in his power to assure the safe passage of the dead from this world to eternal bliss. The priest of the snake claims no more power than does the other priest, nor does he charge any more for what he does claim to do; but he is shrewd enough to prove his power by an occasional poisoning or some other form of sickness-producing magic, and also

THE CROWD CONTINUED TO GROW EVEN MORE FRANTIC.

he works their love of noise, the dance, hot rum, and a general orgie, into his ceremonials. The noise and dancing are both to attract the attention of the snake and to frighten away evil spirits who want to gain possession of the departed soul."

"Is the soul supposed to be safe in heaven when they get through with their shindy?" asked Harry.

"No; it is simply in a place of safety and comfort for the next nine days. If we were here on the ninth night from this, we should witness just such another orgie, save that, as it began without the aid of the Christian priest, it would become disorderly earlier in the evening and would be more of a general drunk before it ended."

CHAPTER XII

CAMP CONTENTMENT

Luxuriant Vegetation — The Cocoanut-palm — The Useful Bamboo — Gorgeous Butterflies — The Butterfly Gun — A Coveted Rarity — Ladder Building — The Moth Beacon — A Weird Sight — Giant Bats — *Loup-garoos* or Vampires — A Midnight Experience — A Rich Harvest — Humming-birds — A Tiny Songster — Scientific Names

"DOCTOR, the further we go into this wonderland the more I find to surprise me in the plants and trees," said Ned. "Are all tropical lands as overgrown with all sorts of vegetation as this island?"

"Not all," was the reply; "some lands are so poorly supplied with rain that they are but scantily covered with growth, but most tropical countries are as densely provided as this and many much more so. What impresses you the most in the plant-life of the island, Ned?"

"The bamboos and palms, I think; although the air-plants and the ferns are about as wonderful. I think the first two, however, are of much more use to mankind, are they not?"

"Undoubtedly they are! It has been said that if a man was landed on a desert island where there was nothing but cocoanut-palms he need feel no fear of death. From that tree he can derive food, shelter, clothing, fuel, building-materials, fibres, paper, sugar, oil, wine, and a host of minor products. From its nut, the milk and jelly of which you boys never seem to tire of, can also be made an excellent oil, a fair wine, and a not bad sugar. From the covering of the outer husk excellent fibres for hats, mats, twines, hammocks, beddings, and clothing can be made. The trunk will make good canoes, fine firewood, and excellent building-materials; while the best of roofs and fair walls can be made of the giant leaves. Certainly a man so placed could keep life going with the aid of this tree until he had started an orchard of native fruits, and from it he could manufacture the lines, arrows, and bows with which animals and fish could be made to contribute to the variety of the table. The cocoanut-palm has well been termed the prince among trees, and the great explorer Von Humboldt gave it as his opinion that it was of more universal value to the people who enjoyed its possession than was any other single product of the animal, vegetable, or mineral kingdoms to any people in the world."

"Bamboos seem almost as useful, with the exception of not affording any food, don't they, Doctor?" asked Harry.

"Perhaps they may be said to stand next in importance," the Doctor said. "Although the omission of food is a great one. In addition to the cocoanut, there are also the date and sago palms, besides a large number of kinds having excellent fruits, but not well known outside of tropical lands. And the Haitian emblem of liberty, the Cabbage Palm, also furnishes a food that these natives value much. But as the 'cabbage' is the end bud of the tree, the removal of which leads to its death, it is a very wasteful sort of food."

"Are palm-trees of the same sort as oaks and pines? Do they live as long?" asked Ned.

"Palms are really of a low order of growth, botanically considered. In some species they do not flower until at an advanced age, immediately after which they die, just as does any annual plant, wheat or corn for example."

"What are some of the best uses of bamboo, Doctor?" asked Ned.

"I need hardly mention house-building, I suppose," the Doctor replied. "You have had hundreds of examples of how the whole house, except the palm-leaf roof, is made from bamboo, and you know enough of their interiors to know that tables, chairs, cradles, cups, saucers, water-jars, and even cooking-utensils are made from this useful grass; for it is only a mammoth grass, after all. Then it can be used to make suspension bridges, pavements for muddy paths, the best of ladders; and very good fences and water-pipes can also be made of it."

"How high are some of these giant grasses, as you call them?" asked Ned.

"I judge some are quite 85 or 90 feet high, that we have thus far seen. In some countries, notably in India, they have been measured to be 230 feet high and 14 inches through at the base, and from some of these mammoth kinds the inhabitants of the Pacific islands make canoes by simply splitting a suitable length in two, each half making a canoe that will hold two men."

This conversation took place at "Camp Contentment," as Ned had named their camp on the south shore of Laguna Enriquillo which, after several days of tedious work, much of which consisted of walking along paths that were little better than the beds of streams, they had reached, well tired out and quite content to spend five or six days there in resting and studying Nature in one of its most attractive spots. The point where they were encamped was a charming one. Back of them was the almost impenetrable wall of the dense woods, through much of which only cutting the way with an axe or cutlass would make it possible to proceed, and then only at a rate of perhaps an eighth of a mile per hour. In front of them were the placid, blue waters of the lake and beyond on the far side another wall of impassable verdure. There was nothing to indicate that there was a living soul within a hundred miles of them. As Ned well said, he felt as completely as did Robinson Crusoe the right to say:—

"I am monarch of all I survey,
My rights there are none to dispute."

Butterflies, their principal coveted treasures, were here most abundant; nowhere else had such a number of species and such hordes of certain kinds been seen by them. One beautiful variety, a combination of azure blue and mother-of-pearl, glinting and flashing like a cluster of rare gems in the sunlight, was especially common on the sand at the margin of the lake. When a group of these exquisite creatures, perhaps two or three hundred in number, flew up in one glistening mass on the approach of the collector, the sight was one never to be forgotten, and Harry expressed it as his opinion that a shower of diamonds could not be more surprisingly and entrancingly beautiful. But the moist sand and the low-growing flowers did not by any means attract all the beauties that they longed for or that they caught glimpses of. Many a rare species made its presence known only by sailing lazily overhead, perhaps seventy-five feet or more from the ground. Often they would catch sight of one particular kind quite six inches across the wings, sailing around more like a bird than a butterfly, which the Doctor told them was probably the rarest species found in the island; not rare in fact, he explained to them, but rare in collections, simply because it was so nearly impossible ever to get a chance to reach it with the longest net handle that could be wielded. In some cases in the Amazonian forests the Doctor had used a gun made to shoot water-cartridges, he told them; a gun in which, after thoroughly greasing the cartridge shell, water was put in the place of shot, and from which it was fired in a solid globule which, if it hit the butterfly, stunned it so that it fell to the ground, where it could usually be captured before it regained its powers of flight. But he had not thought it worth while to bring such a gun on this expedition, though he would certainly do so if he ever had the pleasure of taking them to South America, as he hoped he might.

For two days Harry, rather the more enthusiastic collector of the two, had given much of his time to watching these royal creatures with longing eyes, as they sailed around far out of his reach. On the morning of the third day he came to the Doctor in breathless haste, saying:—

"Oh, Doctor, come with me quick! I have found a tree, the top of which is full of flowers and there must be quite twenty-five of those beautiful *Papilios* sucking honey from them. If we can only climb to the top, I know we can get at least a dozen, at any rate."

When the Doctor saw the spot that Harry had discovered, which was a vast cluster of the flowers of a climbing-plant that had grown quite to the top and all over the central limb of a mighty forest monarch, he exclaimed:—

"Well, Harry, you couldn't have found a worse place to get up to for miles around. Why, that first limb is sixty feet from the ground, and two of us, holding each other's hands, could hardly reach around the trunk; then how do you suppose we can ever get into the top, which must be quite 140 feet from the ground? If you will tell me how, we will try your plan, if it is safe."

"Can't we make some sort of an arrangement with vegetable ropes; or can't Dave or Henri tell us some way to climb into it?" asked Harry, looking much disappointed.

For answer the Doctor walked back to the tent, where dinner was being prepared, and asked each of the black men if he knew any way to climb to the top of such a tree; but each assured him that it could not be done. This was very disappointing to Harry and to Ned also, when he had been with his brother to gaze up at the idly-sailing prizes, so far from their reach. During the dinner both boys were very quiet, each evidently being busy racking his brain in an attempt to invent some sure method of scaling that mighty height; but when dinner was over and the Doctor put the question again to them, all four were compelled to admit that the problem appeared to be too hard to be solved.

"Well, if you all give the puzzle up, I will show you a plan that I saw in use in Borneo and that I have used in Brazil and Venezuela frequently, by which we shall be in the top of that tree before four hours have passed. Ordinarily so much trouble as we are now going to take is hardly worth while, but as we shall be here two or three days longer and as those butterflies are so valuable that a dozen of them will sell for enough to pay the expenses of our entire trip into the interior, I think it worth while in this case."

So saying, the Doctor commissioned Dave to cut him five stout bamboo poles about forty feet long and not less than four inches in diameter; and Henri he told to bring him several hundred feet of strong, flexible vegetable ropes. The boys he sent out to cut about fifty bamboo sticks from one and one-half to two and one-half inches thick and thirty inches long, telling each of the messengers to bring the first fourth part of his task to the tree to be climbed, as soon as he had finished it. When Ned and Harry arrived with a dozen of their bamboo sticks, they found the Doctor already cutting notches at regular intervals in a bamboo pole that Dave had brought, while on the ground lay a pile of vegetable ropes cut into four-foot lengths. The Doctor was inclined to be non-committal, and they went away after more sticks, much mystified.

When they came back with the next arm-load of sticks, however, the Doctor's plan was instantly plain to them; for he was already about twenty feet in the air on a stout ladder, one side of which was the tree and the other one of Dave's poles. Having stood the latter upright by the tree and about two feet from it, he tied it fast to two of the bamboo sticks which, after pointing their hard ends, he had driven deep into the bark of the tree. The outer ends of these sticks fitted into notches cut in the upright pole, and in that position they had been firmly tied with the pieces of vegetable rope. These first two rounds of a ladder which would finally reach into the tree-top held the pole so securely, that, after another was in place, the Doctor could stand on the lower one, and, steadying himself against the other two, drive a fourth into place and tie it, in turn. Thus he went up two feet at a time, so that by the time he was thirty feet from the ground he had a ladder almost as firm as the tree into which one side of it was securely driven; and from that point he had Dave reach up another pole which he tied with great care to the lower one, their ends overlapping ten feet and the notches in each coming together so that the next three or four rounds would help bind both the more firmly.

As he promised them, by the time five o'clock had arrived, although it was after one o'clock when they started to work, they were able to climb up 120 feet into the tree, at which point the limbs were so placed that they had little difficulty in reaching the highest possible point. This was an engineering triumph that delighted the boys and brought forth many words of praise from Dave and an expression of wondering admiration on the face of Henri that was odd to behold. But the Doctor was not satisfied with the ladder alone, for he set at once to work sawing off some of the top limbs in such a way as not to interfere with the growth of the flower-covered vines that were so attractive to the butterflies. Across the top of these limbs he firmly tied stout bamboo cross-pieces that he had had Dave cut, and over these he tied others in such a way as to make a firm platform about twelve feet square, on which three persons could stand at one time, very securely, although there was, of course, a certain amount of vibration from the tree itself. It was nearly dark when the last floor bamboo was in place, and as the Doctor and the boys came down the ladder, Ned said,

"This is the biggest thing that has happened to us yet. I can hardly wait for to-morrow morning to come; I want to get up there and catch those glorious Papilios so much."

"You will not have to wait until to-morrow morning," the Doctor replied. "I propose that we make a moth beacon on that platform to-night; we have spent too much time on the job not to utilize it now in every possible way."

After supper, while the boys were getting together nets, bottles, boxes, and jars for a raid on the moths, the Doctor took from their belongings a white sheet, brought for collecting purposes and not for bedding, as they always slept rolled up in blankets, and prepared a bundle of shaved sticks that Dave had brought in at the Doctor's request. When all was ready they proceeded to the tree, where the Doctor made them remove their shoes and stockings, as a bamboo floor so far above the ground was far too slippery and treacherous to wear shoes on.

When they were all three on top he began by putting each of the boys in a harness of vegetable rope, passed around the body over the hips and under the arms, and this he fastened firmly by another rope, about six feet long, to the middle of the platform. The excitement of moth-catching was much too great to run any risk of their chasing a coveted prize over the edge of a platform 140 feet from the ground. Then he spread the sheet over one corner of the platform so as to cover about one quarter of it; next he tied the bundle of shaved sticks or fagots to a bamboo pole about six feet long, and this he secured in a nearly upright position at the edge of the platform near the sheet, leaning it somewhat forward so that anything burning that dropped from it would fall into the tree and not on the platform. Finally, when everything else was ready, he set fire to the bundle of fagots, and in a few moments the tree-tops for a hundred yards around were brightly lit up. The sight was a strange and weird one and, as Harry said, if there were any natives living within a half-dozen miles they would think the last day had come, if they saw that bright light so high in the trees and the three shadowy forms dancing around under it.

There was not much time for comment on the general effect of the experiment, however, for the particular effect for which it had been arranged soon became manifest, as beetle after beetle and moth after moth began hovering around the light and, growing tired, lit on the brilliant white surface of the sheet. Of course, some of the things that they captured as they slowly circled around or after they lit on the sheet were ruined by having flown into the flame, but most of them were not, and the count they made that night of moths and the estimate of beetles showed that they had added over 600 specimens to their treasures, among which were many very rare and some entirely new species. But they were not the only collectors of these trophies, as they soon found; for around and over them and often perilously near the light, there circled several bats of two or three kinds, one of them of a species quite fifteen inches across the wings. This big fellow must have been closely chasing a moth that Ned made a stroke at, for both went into the net at once and it was only by hitting the bat a death-blow on the head that it was prevented from tearing its way out. When it was spread on the platform, with its wide-open mouth, filled with savage-looking little teeth, lending it an appearance of danger, Ned said,

"That's enough to give one the shivers. Why, I should think a thing like that could fly at a man and tear his face open, if it wanted to. Couldn't it, Doctor?"

"No doubt such a creature could do much harm, if it were forced to by being brought into close quarters with a man; but as it is a cowardly animal, subsisting entirely on insects, it is not likely to attempt such a thing. This particular bat, however, is a species to which is ascribed terrible power, for it is one of the kind known hereabouts as *Loupgaroos* or Vampire-bats. Originally, and even yet among some of these blacks, the vampire was believed to be a dead man who had returned in the bodily shape, and who wandered around doing all the mischief he could, including the sucking of the blood from persons asleep. Usually, however, they believe that the vampires are the spirits of the evilly-disposed dead, returned to earth in the form of these monster bats and capable of sucking the blood from a person until death results; and wonderful are the tales they have to tell of their fearful powers. It is not fair to consider these ignorant blacks as the only people who are the victims of such superstition, for in many parts of our own country and especially in Eastern Europe this belief is still quite prevalent. In Greece and Turkey popular faith in vampires remains unshaken to this day. Byron availed himself of this when he wrote the blood-curdling curse in his 'Giaour,' in which the following lines occur:—

> "'But first on earth as vampire sent,
> Thy corse shall from its tomb be rent,
> Then ghastly haunt thy native place,
> And suck the blood of all thy race.'"

"I have found," continued the Doctor, "very well educated blacks in these islands, who could not be brought to doubt the existence of these mythical creatures. The most ignorant all believe in them, thinking that every night at the first cock-crow, about nine or ten o'clock, the *loupgaroos* leave their graves, hasten to a near-by silk-cotton tree and by some mysterious process divest themselves of their skins, which they fold up and carefully hide away. It is largely on this account that it is so perfectly safe to leave any thing, or to camp, under a tree of this kind, because no black man will venture under it at night. When they are rid of their skin, they can either retain their living forms, assume that of a great bat, or become a ball of fire, or in other words, they take the often-seen will-o'-the-wisp to be a vampire in magic form.

Of course, all these firmly held superstitions are made the means of fooling and defrauding the poor blacks by the Vaudoux priests, who let no chance escape whereby they may exact a penny from their dupes for removing such evil spirits as these."

"Then don't the big bats ever do any harm?" asked Harry.

"Yes, sometimes they develop a fondness for blood and become very annoying, even dangerous, to horses and cattle. In a few cases they have been known to suck blood from man, but such are rather rare. I was once assured by a friend who was with me spending some time at a deserted house in a tropical wilderness, that he had suddenly waked up during the night before, feeling sure that a bat had been preparing to suck his blood, as he felt something tugging at one of his feet, and there was a drop of blood on one of his toes and some blood on the foot of the bed when he struck a match. As I was inclined to laugh at him, he asked me to exchange beds with him on the following night, which I did. After trying to keep awake, yet perfectly motionless for a long time, I finally dropped asleep only to wake with a start and a feeling that something had been at my foot. I prepared myself with a cigar-lighting box and propping myself partially up in bed, so that I could see all that happened, and holding the box ready to make a light instantly, I remained quiet for a long and tedious time. Suddenly, again came the tugging at my toe, and when the flash of the cigar-lighter followed instantly, I clearly saw a big hungry-looking rat attempting to gnaw at my foot. So much for one vampire."

The next morning, after the usual hour or two needed to prepare and pack the captures of their previous night, the party repaired to the tree-platform and for three hours, with varying success, laid siege to the beautiful butterflies for whose especial capture the ladder had been erected. These they could not take in the easy fashion possible with the moths, as the day-flies were wary and easily scared away to the clumps of their favorite flowers in adjoining tree-tops, of which there were several near by. Consequently they had to retire part way down the ladder out of sight in the tree-top, every few moments, and there wait until the forgetful creatures came back to their chosen haunts. This strategy, however, repeated each morning that they remained at this camp, resulted in the capture of over a dozen perfect examples of this superb species and more than as many more of those less perfect, but still salable, together with a considerable number of other species of rarity only second to the *Papilios*. So successful were they, that the Doctor said that if, when they reached Jamaica, they could find another such locality they would be able to pay the entire cost of their trip from the proceeds of the sale of butterflies alone, leaving the profits of the other collections as a clean gain.

The butterflies were not all that were valuable to them in this tree-top collecting, however. Humming-birds, of several kinds, were attracted to these heavily-scented flowers, and on their second ascent to the platform the Doctor had them prepared with cartridges for their guns, loaded with "dust-shot," the finest shot made and intended especially for such tiny game. Taking care to shoot these beautiful creatures only when they were where they could easily be picked out of the tangled vines with a long bamboo pole with a three-pronged wire hook on it, they managed to add a number of specimens, both charming and rare, to their fast-swelling collections. One beauty, larger than the others, had a glistening, emerald-green back and white throat, and the Doctor called it *Lampornus Dominicus*, which Harry said was quite enough of itself to kill it without having to shoot at it.

Another species, much smaller and less brilliantly colored, was so tiny and so graceful that the boys were glad when the Doctor told them that it was too common a species to make it worth while to shoot any more of them than they needed for their own private collection. They were doubly glad of this when one of the tiny little fairies, seeming hardly bigger than a big bumblebee, perched carelessly on a near-by twig, and, cocking its head on one side, uttered a succession of tiny "tweep tweeps" that were evidently intended for a song, though it amounted to nothing more than "tweep-tweep-tweep-tweep-toodle-loodle-loodle-tweep" repeated over and over in only two tones for nearly a minute. But it was such a surprising thing from such a tiny songster, and *Mellisuga minima*, as the Doctor called it, seemed to enjoy the performance so much that Ned exclaimed, —

"Well, I'm glad we don't need to shoot those little darlings, but I wish we could take three or four home alive. Would that be possible?"

"No. Humming-birds are of the very essence of freedom and unrestrained airiness, and it has thus far been impossible to keep them in confinement. In a few days, in spite of the best of care, they pine away and die."

"How is it, Doctor," asked Harry, "that the smaller the creature the bigger the name the naturalists have given it? The great lion is only *Felis leo*, four syllables, while one of the smallest butterflies we have in the North is *Polyommatus pseudargiolus*, ten syllables."

"You boys surely understand that the Latin or scientific names given to the animal and plant world are merely given to distinguish the varieties from each other, and the Latin language is chosen because it is more universally understood among well-educated people than any other. Naturally, when the founder of what is known as the modern classification, the naturalist Linné, or Linneus, to Latinize his name, came to give names, he chose, as far as possible, names already in common use in Latin. Thus, as the lion belonged to the cat tribe, he called its genus *Felis*, and gave the name for lion, *leo*, as the specific one. When he came to the principal butterflies, he gave them the Latin name for butterfly, *Papilio*, but when it became necessary to divide the hundreds of species found all over the world into different genera, names were usually devised that indicated some peculiarity common to all the species in a genus. Thus the butterflies having silver spots beneath were arranged in the genus *Argynnis*, which signifies that, and those that are like wood brownies or little satyrs, under the genus *Satyrus*, while those tiny ones that have a profuse sprinkling of small round spots beneath are placed in the genus you have just inquired about, under the appropriate name of *Polyommatus*. The specific or species name is less reasonably applied, as it is sometimes given in honor of its discoverer, or on account of the locality where found. But in the species you mentioned, it was for a long time supposed to be the same as a common European species, called *argiolus*, and when found to be distinct was naturally called *pseudargiolus*, or 'supposed *argiolus*.' So you see these names have their meaning, and often the name alone will help the student to identify a species. As you both become more familiar with Latin, these long formidable-sounding names will lose their terrors for you, and in very many cases, on hearing a new name, you will detect something in it to give you a clue to its owner's characteristics."

"I am glad you made this so plain," said Ned, "for now I'll take more interest in Latin; and I'll no longer think there is no excuse for such terrible names as some of our captures have to bear."

CHAPTER XIII

ABOVE THE CLOUDS

Anticipations — Mountain Heights — An Unattempted Feat — Difficult Mountaineering — An Ideal Camp — Harry's Description of a Mountain View — Planting the Flag — Frost in the Tropics — A Mountain Sunrise — The Inscription above the Clouds — Attacked by a Wild Boar — Excellent Marksmen — A Still More Luxuriant Wilderness — Cannibalism — American versus French Republicanism — Haitian Dignitaries

THE camp by Laguna Enriquillo proved to be so pleasant and so profitable that the boys' stay was delayed for three days beyond their schedule. This suited the lads very well, and they would have willingly prolonged the free and easy life for any indefinite period, had not the Doctor reminded them that already about six weeks of their allotted vacation were gone and they would have to take a very hurried view of Jamaica as it was, and none at all if they did not hurry along on their mapped-out route.

"Is Jamaica any more interesting or a better collecting-field than this?" asked Harry.

"It is not nearly so interesting in the matter of collecting such material as can be pinned in boxes, folded in papers, or put into alcohol. But in the collection of facts, especially such facts as have to do with the study of man, it is a very different field and therefore interesting in another way. While the impressions of black savagery are still fresh in your mind from life here, I want you, and it was your father's wish also, to see what a degree of excellence black civilization can reach under favorable conditions and how high it has reached under English rule in Jamaica. Neither your father nor I had any idea that you were both going to make such famous young naturalists and explorers, imagining that, in common with most travellers, you would want to be moving on constantly to new scenes and excitements. Therefore we expected that four weeks would suffice for the Bahamas and Haiti, and that there would be three weeks for Jamaica and possibly enough time left for a glimpse of the eastern coast of Central America. Now we shall do well to get the three weeks in Jamaica, and must leave the mainland for another trip some day, perhaps next summer, if we want to get back in time for Christmas. I told your father of our change of plan in my last letter from Port au Prince, and I expect we shall get a reply while we are in Kingston, Jamaica. Then we shall know whether your school opens after New Year, and whether we must hurry home."

"Oh, we wouldn't want to miss Christmas at home, anyhow; would we, Ned?" asked Harry.

"No. You see, Doctor, we always have a roaring good time then, and we have never been away from home on Christmas. Even if we had more time here, we could go home in six days and come back after Christmas week, couldn't we?" responded Ned.

"Yes, you could, of course; but that sort of thing costs money. It would at least take $300 to take us all home and back here."

"Father wouldn't mind that when he sees how much we have collected," said Ned. "He said, you remember, that what we collected should belong to all three of us to use as we saw fit."

"I guess there'll be no trouble about arrangements," the Doctor said, with a smile. "No doubt we shall see Christmas and ice and snow at home."

"It's pretty hard to imagine, though; isn't it?" said Harry, as he wiped the beads of perspiration from his face.

Two days after this conversation they pulled up stakes at "Camp Contentment," and after the hardest travelling they had yet had, they encamped at the foot of La Selle, the tallest of the peaks in the south of the island, and perhaps the highest land in all the West Indies.

"Why don't they know exactly whether it's the highest mountain, or not, Doctor?" asked Ned.

"Because no one has ever been on top of it with any apparatus for assuring its height, and that is true of two other high mountains in this island. The Haitians say that no one has ever been to the top of this mountain, but there is reason to believe that the Spaniards reached the summit about four centuries ago in their eager search for gold. However, by rough triangulation, — a species of surveying at a distance, — it has been estimated at about 9000 feet. That makes it higher than anything else in the West Indies, unless one of the two other principal mountains in this island is higher."

"Can't we climb it, Doctor, and settle the matter, and make them admit that American boys can do what the men of other lands have not cared to try?" asked Harry.

"That remains to be seen, provided you care to try it. It looks to me as though the approach from this side would not be very steep; but, even if we get to the top, we cannot settle the question, as we shall still be ignorant of the heights of the other mountains. We can, however, boast of accomplishing a most difficult task, and with our pocket barometer can come within fifty or one hundred feet of our exact height above the sea. And the experience of hardships and the view will be superior to anything you have yet had."

"That settles it!" said Harry, the enthusiast. "We'll conquer old La Selle, won't we, Ned?"

"We'll make a good struggle for it, anyway," was the response of the other. "But I am more afraid of the horses giving out than anything else."

"We are now camped about as far as we can take them," the Doctor replied. "We will leave them here in charge of Dave and Henri, taking only 'Lisha with us as an extra companion; for we shall have to come back this way to avoid getting lost in these interminable wildernesses."

The next morning, sometime before sunrise, they were off on their upward journey, telling Dave to wait for them until the fourth day or until he heard a signal fired above him, when he was to try to come after them with the strongest horse. The Doctor carried several dynamite cartridges to use as signals, and he told Dave that at least every hundred feet they would cut a gash or "blaze" in a tree or hack down a sapling, so that their route would be plain. But nothing short of a serious accident, a broken leg or something of that sort, would delay them beyond the four days. To the boys it seemed very strange that a climb of perhaps a mile and a half above their present camp should take two days each way, but long before noon had arrived they began to wonder whether the Doctor had allowed enough time.

Previous to this they had had some experience in cutting their way through a jungle at a snail's gait, and twice they had had to unload their horses and help them up steep walls, directly in their path, with ropes and a pully that Dave had brought along. But now they came to a stretch of jungle where they were most of their time waist-deep in vast seas of moss, with a perfect network of giant ferns over them, the taller trees shutting out every ray of sunlight and giving the effect of a perpetual twilight, while thousands of vegetable ropes and unexpected roots impeded every step. Each of them was armed with a *machete*, or cutlass, and took turns in leading and cutting the way, the one next following acting as collector for such things as they could take along under light marching-order, and the rear guard watching to see that plenty of signs were left so that they could easily find their way back or Dave could follow them. Each hour was thus divided: for twenty minutes the Doctor led, for the next ten it was Ned's turn, with the Doctor in the rear, for ten more Harry was the guide, and for the remaining twenty they took the best rest they could get in such a hot, steaming, unventilated jungle, where not a breath of air moved and an overpowering odor of decaying vegetation was most depressing.

After seven hours of this sort of thing, and when the boys were about ready to hint that it was a bigger contract than they had supposed, the jungle suddenly began to thin out; here and there was to be seen a patch of sunlight overhead, and the air was perceptibly cooler and occasionally a slight puff of quite cold air, it seemed in contrast, blew over them. They were on a narrow ridge, the back of which was not more than thirty feet wide, the sides sloping away precipitously and giving views of enormously deep valleys on both sides, with an open view to the south, over some miles of hills and valleys and the ocean beyond. Here, the Doctor's barometer told them, they were about 6000 feet above the sea, and he thought that the next 1000 feet ought to bring them to a good camp for the night, as it was hardly prudent to spend the first night on top, on account of the sudden change from the hot-house temperature of the jungle to the frost-line atmosphere of the summit. Before they had gone 500 feet further in elevation they were brought face to face with a deep chasm, to bridge which was impossible and in which they decided to camp. For at the bottom there was pure drinking-water from a mountain rivulet, and the sides of the ravine acted as barriers for much of the cold wind that sprang up after midnight.

The next morning an early start and some very hard climbing over rocky ways — for towards the top the vegetation grew sparser and no longer carpeted all the rocks with two to three feet of moss — brought them at about 11 o'clock to the summit. The impression made on the boys, when they finally conquered the very crown of the mighty peak and reached a point where the view burst upon them from every direction, was far beyond their powers of expression. Harry's words, used in a letter written that night, while all was fresh in his memory, made their feelings about as plain as language can. He wrote: —

"Hurrah and hurrah! Here we are on top of the earth, with everything down in the hollow below us! I write this on top of La Selle, perhaps the highest mountain in the West Indies or in North America east of the Rocky Mountains. We are 8923 feet above the Caribbean Sea, which is around us on three sides and looks like a saucer of blue china, while we sit on a lump of earth in the middle, with grass all around us. The enormous jungles that we have been slowly cutting our way through for nearly fourteen hours of the hardest work we boys ever tried, look now like fine moss, so far are we above their mighty tree-tops.

"Hip, hip, hurrah, again! We are the first boys who have ever reached so high a point in the whole Caribbean group, and probably the first of any age who have climbed up here since old Columbus's time. We have set a flag flying from a pole tied in a tree-top, and to-night we shall have a monster bonfire going that will be the talk of the whole island for many days to come. No one has any idea that we are in this part of the interior, and the poor, ignorant darkies will think it is either a volcano starting or some sort of work of their Vaudoux gods. Ned and I would rather have had an American flag floating from this point, but we had to rest content with a small Haitian one the Doctor bought in Port au Prince for the purpose. He says we wouldn't like to have a Haitian plant his flag on our Pike's Peak, and of course he is right.

"I wish you at home could see this wonderful view. With the Doctor's telescope we can see mountains over 125 miles away, and the variety of the views on every hand is wonderful. South of us the mountains slope rapidly away to the coast, and we can see the harbor of Jacmel very plainly; as far as the eye can reach to the east is ridge after ridge and valley after valley of the wildest land in Santo Domingo, with the blue waters of the large lake where we have been camping in plain sight. To the north are other mountain chains and the great valley in which lies Port au Prince at the water's edge. And to the west stretches the long arm of Southern Haiti, with many high mountains along its centre. We are above the most of the clouds, and, although at our very feet, as it seems, there are bananas, cocoanut-palms, mangoes, and no end of tropical things, we are quite likely to have frost up here to-night, the Doctor says."

And so it proved to be; for in spite of a thick blanket that each had brought up, strapped to his back, and a rousing fire, of the biggest dried sticks they could carry to it, they spent a rather cold and cheerless night, and it was a welcome sight to them all when there began to come a grayish tinge on the eastern horizon. The Doctor was the first one stirring, and he soon had a roaring fire and a steaming pot of coffee ready to overcome the stiffened limbs and shivering muscles. Before the coffee had disappeared, it began to dawn on the boys that their companion had spoken truly when he said that the first hour or so of the new day would repay them a hundredfold for the toil of their climb and the discomforts of the night. At first it seemed to them that they were on a tiny island in an endless sea of foamy billows; for on every hand and almost up to their feet were fleecy clouds, with nothing else whatever to be seen. Then slowly, as the light began to redden in the east, these billows of the upper air receded and here and there the top of some near-by peak appeared above them like an island suddenly heaved up by the sea.

By rare good fortune it proved to be a clear day that was dawning, and when at last the sun rose out of the eastern billows of cloud, looking like an enormous disk of burnished copper, it gilded the top and edges of every cloud and tinged with red every mountain top, until they seemed to be on one of a score or more of ruby-colored islands in a sea of gold and gray. Then, little by little, the sun's heat melted the clouds away, and valley after valley changed, under their very eyes, from the dark of night to the gray of dawn and the bright glare of day, a transformation scene that so entranced the boys that they lost all sight of the time. While they were enjoying it to the fullest extent the Doctor, to whom such views were an old story, although always enjoyable, was busy pounding away at the face of a rock that projected from the surface and was the highest point of the mountain. When they joined him, the boys found that with a big stone as a mallet and a small stone-chisel which he had thoughtfully brought along, he was just putting the finishing touches on an inscription which read: —

THE DAWSON BOYS

Nov. 25, 1892

After a consultation, while they were eating a hearty breakfast, it was decided that as the path was cleared all the way and as they could easily make the downward trip before dark that night, it would be just as well to take it easily and do a little collecting along the route and spend another night at their former camp in the gorge below. They bade good-bye to the splendor of the mountain reluctantly, but a chance kick against a rotting tree trunk that disclosed a horde of beetles of a half dozen sorts caused them to think of other things before they had got two hundred yards downward on their route.

They reached their intended camp in time for dinner, and while the Doctor and Harry were preparing that meal, Ned walked a short distance down the ravine in search of beetles and such other trophies as could easily be put in their alcohol bottles. Suddenly he came back on a run and out of breath, his eyes wide open with fright, exclaiming, as he picked up his gun: —

"Doctor, quick! a monster pig is trying to kill 'Lisha."

"Hold on there, Ned!" was the Doctor's caution. "You have too light shot in that gun for a wild hog. They are very dangerous animals, and we must each go armed and with cartridges that are loaded with buckshot." So saying, he unpacked his knapsack and took from it a double handful of cartridges. Handing a dozen to each of the boys, they all quickly loaded their guns and hurried to the point from which came 'Lisha's hoarse barking and the gruff grunts of the hog. At the base of a tree stood a large, gaunt wild boar, with the bristles on his neck and along his spine standing erect with anger, keeping his hindquarters against the tree and between two buttressed roots and his head always towards 'Lisha, who was thus prevented from gaining a deadly grip on his antagonist by fear of the savage-looking tusks that protruded from the half-open mouth.

The Doctor whispered to the boys to separate a few yards on each side of him and follow his example of slowly closing in on the brute. When they reached a suitable distance he would attract the boar's attention, when, if it was a coward, it would turn to escape, in which case they must not fire at it, as they would be far more apt to hit 'Lisha, who would harass it by biting at its flanks and who would soon bring it to a stand again for another chance for a shot. The chances were even, however, he explained to them, that the brute would rush at one of them in his fury, the moment his attention was attracted. In that case, no matter whom he came towards, all three were to fire at him, and one would be pretty sure to aim a deadly shot. Care must be taken, however, to aim at the forequarters or head, so as not to run any risk of hitting 'Lisha.

The party started cautiously down the gorge towards the hog, which by this time was frantic in its futile efforts to deal 'Lisha a deadly blow, the Doctor in the middle and each boy about twenty-five feet from him on one or the other hand. When they had reached a spot about fifty yards from the brute, the Doctor suddenly shouted to the dog: "Sick him, 'Lisha! sick him!" Without one moment's hesitation, but with the merest glance towards the source of the words, the brute lowered its head, and dashing past 'Lisha, who was now an unimportant consideration, rushed headlong towards the Doctor. For barely a second the boys were dazed by the suddenness of the onslaught, but the sight of the Doctor coolly raising his gun to his shoulder recalled them to their senses, and instantly their guns rang out sharp and in unison. With a bound quite three feet in the air the hog sprang forward, and, just as both boys started to run for trees to climb, fell in a quivering heap and died almost instantly. It was hard to tell which showed the greatest joy, the boys or 'Lisha, but the latter certainly manifested the more hatred as he gnawed and bit his dead foe and barked his deep defiance close to the very teeth he was so apprehensive of but a moment before.

Then came a search for wounds, which were soon found, and much to the delight of the boys the Doctor cried,

"Well done, brave hunters of the fearless wild boar! Evidently neither of you was badly rattled, for here on the left side, at a spot that could only have been reached by Ned's aim, is a wound that breaks the foreshoulder and another that must have gone into the heart. That of course accounts for the instant death. But it was not needed; for here on the other side are two wounds, one of which has severed the jugular vein and the other of which has pierced the cheek bone and entered the brain. Besides these, I find seven more shot wounds, four of which would have brought your game to earth, even if the others had not

INSTANTLY THEIR GUNS RANG OUT SHARP AND IN UNISON.

proved fatal. So I think it is safe to say that either of you can pass muster as an accomplished boar hunter, which is much more than can be said of most boys, or men either, for that matter, as boar hunting is a most hazardous and nerve-trying sport."

"But where do you come in, Doctor? You haven't told us where your shots landed," said Ned.

"Oh, as I thought you two would like to take that boar's head home, to be mounted as a trophy of your bravery, I refrained from firing, so that there could be no doubt as to it being the product of your combined marksmanship. I congratulate each of you on being able to claim to have dealt the brute a deadly wound."

The removal of the skin from the head, cleaning the skull, and cutting up some steaks for the next few meals, occupied the rest of an exhausting day; and, although the young hunters retired quite early, it was unusually late when they arose the next morning, and very nearly dark when they rejoined Dave and Henri, much to the surprise of the latter, a day before they were expected.

The following three days were given up to almost constant travelling down the southern slopes of the La Selle Range on the way to Jacmel, and it was quite late on the night of the third day that they reached that dilapidated town. On this part of their trip they encountered nothing of an unusual nature, save that the sunny exposure seemed to make this side of the range appear more tropical, and there was some change in the kinds of animal life they encountered. Some of the birds especially attracted their attention and their shots as well. Flocks of gorgeous trogons, with an iridescent green head and back, dull lilac throat, royal scarlet breast, and deep green tail, with black and white mottlings on it and the wings, occasionally made some clump of woodland glisten with their wondrous combination of colors, and vibrate with their harsh, inharmonious notes. Not only as a species of value to their collections, but as an excellent source of food, they found the abundance of a robin-like bird, which the Doctor called *Mimocichla ardesiaca*, very fortunate. In the early mornings their sleep was disturbed by flocks of a medium-sized green parrot, the same kind that is commonest in Northern cages; and immense flocks of a beautiful white-crowned pigeon afforded them another supply of delicious food. Here, too, there was a greater abundance of snakes, though very few were poisonous, and the species of the lizard tribe seemed to be without number. During one of these nights they were awakened by the not distant barking of dogs, to which 'Lisha responded as lustily as his hoarse bulldog voice would permit. These did not come within sight, and both their guides as well as the Doctor agreed in thinking them to be wild dogs. These, the latter explained to them, were, like the wild hogs, descendants of those brought here in the early days of the Spanish occupancy, now running wild and as fierce and dangerous as their original savage progenitors. In these forests, also, the Doctor pointed out to them, growing wild and yet bearing luxuriantly, only to have their products rot on the ground, cotton, Indian corn, tobacco, cacao, ginger, indigo, arrowroot, bananas, pineapples, artichoke, sweet potatoes, and mango trees at almost every step. Yet with all this vegetable wealth, unexcelled anywhere in the world, Haiti is yearly growing poorer and poorer, more and more degraded and savage.

Jacmel the lads found to be about such another spot as their first Haitian harbor, Port à Paix, but perhaps a little more squalid and uncivilized. They learned that they would have at least two days to wait for the Royal Mail steamer on its way from Barbadoes to Jamaica, and the time was mainly occupied in becoming acquainted with some of the foremost white and mulatto residents of the town and in packing many of their captures so as to ship them directly home. Here Dave and Henri bade them good-bye, taking an overland route with the horses back to Port au Prince. The former parted with them very reluctantly, but liberal presents from each of them, with gifts to be carried to Henriette, and the promise that if they returned to this part of the world to explore parts of Central or South America he should be sent for to join them, did much to reconcile him.

From one of their new acquaintances, a well-to-do native merchant, it was learned that there had recently been much reason to think that the Vaudoux superstitions were on the increase in the interior, and that there was much talk, in a hushed way, of the increase in cannibalism among the most degraded of the peasantry. The practice of "wanga," a term indicating the use of charms, philters, and poisons, was on the increase, and there had been a number of sudden deaths due, without much doubt, to the use of deadly poisons by the Vaudoux priests. It was well-nigh impossible to get the police authorities to act in such cases, as there were few of them, from officers to judges, who were not more or less under the influence of the degrading superstition. That young children had recently been so poisoned by their nurses as to appear to be dead, had then been buried, only to be secretly dug up again to be restored to life and then given over to these bloodthirsty priests to be used as a sacrifice and afterwards eaten, he felt sure. But there was no use of telling these things to the authorities, for he and others who thought as he did of these horrors would simply be spotted by the snake worshippers and be in constant danger of their lives.

When the Doctor expressed his sympathy with him at this deplorable condition of his beautiful land, he replied,

"Ah! we poor Haitians made our great mistake years ago, long before my time. Had we taken your Washington and not the Napoleon of France as our model, had we looked to the American institutions of freedom and justice instead of aping French manners and Parisian bombast, we might have long ago become a greater people."

"Is it true, Doctor, that this terrible cannibalism is in this island, now?" Ned asked, after their guest had left them.

"I am very sorry to have to say that it undoubtedly is, Edward," was his reply. "It seems that a century of republican freedom, so called, and the blessings of religion, and an unexcelled climate and soil ought to have produced great improvements in this people; but that they are going backwards towards the savagery from which they were brought in Africa every fair-minded man who has studied them on the spot believes. Nowhere in the world is the poisoner's art better understood to-day than here. The profession that began centuries ago with the use of snake's poison on a spear-point or decayed flesh smeared on an arrow-head, has improved until, from strychnine, which they extract from the wild plant, *Strychnos toxifera*, up through a long line of native and introduced poisons, they are able to produce the exact effect and just at the time that is desired in any special case."

It was a great contrast, after their weeks of freedom from restraint, to be again on the deck of an ocean liner; but the refinements of their surroundings and the class of passengers and officers they were soon acquainted with on the Royal Mail Line steamship "Atrata," reconciled them to the change. All the rest of the day they sailed in close view of the ironbound coast of the long southwestern arm of Haiti, passing only the uncertain port of Aux Cayes in all that long stretch, and seeing but few other signs of life for over 150 miles; and as the sun set the last they saw of the beautiful but superstition-ridden island was the gilded dome of La Hotte, a lofty mountain towering a mile above the sea, and the centre of a part of the island, the Doctor told them, that was even worse in wildness and in degradation than any they had seen. As they passed Aux Cayes an elderly clergyman on board told them of an amusing experience of his some years before at that port. He had been sent there on missionary work and came well introduced, so that the mayor of the town, a black, gorgeous in cheap gold braid and a showy uniform, but with nearly bare feet and naked ankles, called on him with much formality.

On the next day he saw this same gentleman led off to the town lockup to be detained over night, for, as he was the principal cook of the place as well as its mayor and much given to prolonged sprees, the "General" of that region had thought it best thus to capture him and make sure of his sobriety on the morrow, when he was under contract to produce a state dinner for his chief. At this same town their informant had also seen a resplendent individual, who was frequently on the street in blue coat, white trousers, a cockaded hat, a sword, and not a few medals, but with bare feet, accosted with every mark of distinguished consideration. Taking it for granted that here was some eminent citizen, he made inquiry as to his identity, and was informed that he was "Monsieur, le Gardien de les Boeufs"; or, in our less high-sounding English, the town's pound-keeper and catcher of stray cattle.

CHAPTER XIV

THE NEGRO'S PARADISE

Jamaica, the Blest — Port Royal — A History of Guilt — The Earthquake's Vengeance — A Miraculous Escape — A Famous Hurricane — Pelicans — Quashie Lingo — Street Sights — The Jamaica Museum — Modified Negro Rule — Thoughts of Home — King's House — Sir Henry and Lady Blake — Luxuriance of Life in the Tropics — An Ideal Winter Resort — Troops in Cloudland — Chased by a Storm

WHEN they came on deck the next morning Ned and Hal found the Doctor looking towards the coast that they were skirting, a low, sandy shore, backed by a plain gradually ascending to where steep foothills rose into a majestic mountain range not many miles in the interior. Seeing the boys, one on each side of him, he said,

"There, boys, is one of the loveliest spots in all God's beautiful earth. Some of the most glowing descriptions ever penned by experienced travellers have been written of Jamaica, and no one who has tasted of the plenty of its fertile valleys or experienced the genial climate of its hills, ever feels quite content again in the bleak north. In all my travels I have never seen a region where I have felt that I could spend my days in greater contentment than here."

During the conversation that followed, in which the Doctor pointed out the mountain region which they were soon to visit, the breakfast gong sounded, and when they came out on deck again they were just rounding a narrow point of land and coming to a temporary halt in front of Port Royal, while the customs authorities and the port physician came on board to go through the necessary formalities. While the ship's papers were being examined to see that there was no possibility of yellow fever or other contagion on board, the Doctor was telling the boys something of the early history of the low-lying, uninviting town, that appeared to have only one church, but an abundance of barracks and naval storehouses in it, with some low, forbidding looking fortresses beyond it to seaward.

From the earliest days of the Spanish conquest and extermination of the peaceful Arrowack natives who were the inhabitants of Jamaica, the harbor now known as Kingston Harbor had been recognized as one of the safest naval ports in the world, and this point of land at its entrance was early settled as the key to the whole south side of the island, for whoever owned "Puerto Real" controlled that harbor, and through it the fast growing capital of the island, San Jago de la Vega. Thus it naturally came that Port Royal grew to be the principal town of the island, and in time the chief city of the West Indies, when the buccaneers and freebooters discovered its merits as a safe harbor for their vessels. When the island succumbed to General Venables and Admiral Penn, father of our own good William Penn, and it became an English colony under the direction of Oliver Cromwell and his Roundhead parliament, there was little change in Port Royal. Save that the ships that sailed into it, laden with booty wrested from the mainlands or seized by piracy on the high seas, flew the English flag and proceeded against the ships of Spain and France, instead of the reverse, as had so long been the case, the scenes of unlawful carnage and unholy thirst for gain were much as before. Storehouses were bursting with the cloths and silks of Europe's choicest looms and the wines and luxuries that had been sent out to colonial governors and nabobs, but that had fallen into the hands of licensed British piracy and found their way to the city, which towards the close of the 17th century grew to be known as the richest and wickedest spot of land of its size in all the earth.

Finally there came a day in the history of this wicked town, a day that could well be called a Day of Judgment, when on a beautiful Sabbath morning, at about the time the few church-goers were on their homeward way, a quivering of the ground was felt; and before they had time to seek places of shelter, the roofs began to topple upon them, and with one convulsive throb a great part of the town went down under the surging force of a mighty tidal wave. Following quickly came another convulsion of the earthquake, and where, but a moment before, had stood the best and most prosperous part of the town were forty feet of the troubled waters of the bay. The divers say that even yet they can find signs, after all these 200 years, of the overwhelmed city, now richly overgrown with coral and sponge; and there are not a few Jamaicans who are blessed with such imaginations that, on very clear days when the water is least in motion, they profess to be able to see signs of the submerged scene of wealth and luxury over the sides of their boats.

"How many people were drowned?" asked Ned, after the Doctor had told them this.

"Thousands upon thousands; and not only here, but throughout the whole island, in every part of which the destructiveness of the earthquake was felt. So many were killed here that the floating corpses in the harbor brought the yellow fever, and for a time it looked as though this cause would kill as many as the earthquake had. Few survived in the submerged part of the city, and of the few who did by far the most famous was the man who now lies buried over on the opposite side of the harbor at Green Bay. His gravestone tells to this day that he had been out to buy a live rooster for dinner, and that when the first tidal wave overtook him and he went down he forgot, in his agony, to let go the bird; and when the second shock was followed by another enormous wave, he was thrown high and dry upon the land with the rooster still firmly held in his hand, neither of them being much the worse for their terrible experience. It was more than forty years afterward that he was laid at rest at Green Bay."

While these facts had been engrossing the boys' thoughts the port physician had passed the vessel, and they were in a little while well on their way to the Kingston docks, six miles away on the north shore of the bay. The Doctor called their attention to the spaciousness of this land-locked bay, stating that while it was quite capable of sheltering the combined navies of the world and was claimed by many to be one of the five finest harbors in the world, it was so protected by coral reefs at its mouth that no vessel could hope to enter it safely against the fire of the forts at Port Royal. Yet its placid loveliness as they now sailed in, he explained, was by no means indicative of what was possible when a West Indian hurricane swept over it. In earlier days, when Kingston was the metropolis of all these islands, a hurricane had suddenly turned its quiet waters into a sea of foaming billows, masthead high, and when the storm subsided over one hundred vessels of various kinds and sizes had sunk to be covered with the palaces built up by corals, sponges, and *zoöphytes*.

As they steamed up the harbor scores of pelicans were to be seen sitting lazily on the buoys, while here and there one sailing overhead suddenly folded its wings and darted into the water with great force, always returning to the surface with a captured fish.

"Pelicans always strike the water at an angle and never enter it from an exactly vertical position," said the Doctor. "This is believed to be for the purpose of saving them as much as possible from the terrible strain on their enormous bills as they enter the water with such force and thereby diminishing the shock to their rather slender necks. Although all their feeding is done in the bays and on saltwater fish, they live in the mountains and only seek these waters for food."

Unlike the other harbors the boys had thus far visited in the West Indies, they found Kingston provided with excellent docks; but when their vessel was made fast to one of the best of these and the gang-plank was run out, their vessel was soon boarded by much the same sort of black people as they had seen elsewhere, save that these looked more thrifty and intelligent than the others. But the language that greeted their ears made a most vivid impression on both of the boys from the first, and Harry, turning to the Doctor, said,

"I thought this was an English colony and supposed we should hear English spoken here. What sort of language are these people talking, anyway? I hear some English words, but the most of it is the most ridiculous 'jabberwocky' I've heard yet."

"And the strangest part of it is that they think it is English," the Doctor replied. "Speak to any of them and you will see that your English is understood perfectly, but you will have to be on the island for some time, several months in fact, before you can understand their replies perfectly. Try one with a question, Harry."

Picking out a strapping big, coal-black fellow in a white linen suit, who was talking most vociferously, Harry said,

"How much will you charge to carry my trunk and two satchels to the Custom House wharf? Can you carry them all at once?"

"Hi, Buckrah! I dat quick-quick fe quattie fe de lil' tings, an' tanner fe tunk."

"There you have a fair but a rather easy example of Jamaica negro talk, or 'Quashie dialect,' as it is called," said the Doctor, laughing as he saw Hal's look of bewilderment at the reply his question had received. "What he has tried to make you understand is that he will charge you a 'quattie' or one-quarter of a sixpence (three cents

in our money) for each of your small packages, and a
'tanner' or sixpence for the trunk. Before you have
been here long you will hear even queerer English than
that, especially in the interior."

After the belongings of the party had been passed by the
customs authorities, the Doctor hailed one of the many
cabs that were passing back and forth or standing on nearly
every corner, and for the use of which the very modest
charge of sixpence was made for each person for any distance within the central part of the city, and putting their
satchels in with the boys, their trunks having been sent on
ahead, at the words "Park Lodge!" their horse was off at
a sort of combination between a trot and a canter. As
they moved along through the well-filled streets, in which
there were more pedestrians than vehicles, because most
of the sidewalks were merely porches in front of the business places and were placed at all sorts of inconvenient
levels, the Doctor explained to them that while there were
several very comfortable hotels in Kingston, one of which
made special claims to being quite Northern in its style, he
was going to take them to one of the most cosy of them,
where the creole cooking and typical Jamaica ways would
be a pleasant surprise to them, after their experience with
Haitian cookery and uncleanliness.

This place was found to be towards the outskirts of
the town, surrounded by a high wall and in the midst of a
very charming tropical garden. From this point the lads
found it quite convenient to make trips of exploration into
the heart of the city, and yet they were sufficiently near
enough to some good collecting fields outside of the town

to be able to get to them without attracting undue attention. Among their town trips one of the most interesting was to the museum and library of the Jamaica Institute, where they found a very fair collection of the animal and plant life of the island carefully arranged and well displayed, together with many interesting books pertaining to the island's history and resources, and a fair collection of curiosities and relics. Chief among the latter was the cracked bronze bell that had hung in the church tower at Port Royal at the time of the famous earthquake, and an iron cage with cruel spikes in it, which had been dug up with some human bones in it, and which was known to have been used to hang up slaves alive, so that they could die by slow torment.

A sail across the bay to the naval station, a drive to the military barracks, where the black troops, or "West India Regiments" as they are called, are stationed, a trip on the railway to quaint old Spanishtown, or Saint Jago de la Vega (St. James of the Valley), as it was called for three centuries, and various strolls through the more primitive parts of the city, occupied several days of their rapidly shortening time in a very pleasant way. Their inspection of Kingston was a continued source of surprise to them. They had become so accustomed to negro squalor and wretchedness, so accustomed to think of the negro as a thoroughly unreliable being, after their sojourn in Haiti, that it was hard for them to realize for a time what a difference there was between the negrodom of Port au Prince and that of Kingston. When it did begin to dawn upon them that here, notwithstanding that there were many very idle, worthless blacks among the population, especially among the men, still the general average of industry, cleanliness, and good behavior was quite equal to that of most towns peopled with whites, they saw how well it was that the Doctor had cautioned them against forming their ideas of the negro's chances of advancement from what they saw in Haiti. As they stood on an observation tower one afternoon looking over the clustering houses, all so much like large white boxes, with regular roofs sloping in each direction from a central peak and with their uniform, green "jalousie" blinds, Ned said,

"Really, Doctor, I think this must be a charming place to live in. I don't see but that the few hundred whites in the city manage the place and all its black people quite as well as though they were in the majority. Everything seems as orderly and almost as businesslike as in our own land."

"If it were as you seem to think, that the whites manage the blacks, things might not move on so well, but the fact is that the blacks and browns have the affairs of the town just as much at heart as the whites have, simply because they have precisely the same rights and privileges and all colors govern together. It does me good every time I come to Kingston, simply because I see here, better than anywhere else, how much the black man is capable of under fair treatment, and I realize that he is the coming man in all tropical America. These uniformly hot climates are too hard on the whites for them ever to reach a successful form of civilization here alone; in two or three generations they die out, while the blacks grow and thrive here, and in time will, I feel sure, make of all the region from Cuba to the Amazon one of the world's principal gardens," the Doctor replied.

After a few days of such inspection the party moved out from Kingston to a favorite resort, Constant Springs, where a large hotel under American management was one of the principal attractions of the island, and where their close proximity to the mountains made it possible for them to vary their collecting experiences very much. Here, too, the electric light, with which the hotel was supplied, proved to be very attractive to moths, and many were the rarities that they added each night to their rapidly growing stores. A large bath-house provided with the largest bathing-tank the boys had ever seen was also a great attraction, and they both voted this to be altogether the best place they had yet found for studying tropical nature under the most comfortable circumstances.

When they had first reached the island the lads had found quite a varied collection of letters awaiting their arrival from their parents and sister, and from these they eagerly devoured the news. In a letter to the Doctor their father informed them that the principal of their school had been seriously ill and that it had been decided not to open the school again for some time, perhaps not before the next fall term, if ever at all. Therefore, their parents were willing that they should stay some weeks longer if they so desired, considering the very excellent reports of their behavior that the Doctor had made. In reply to this the Doctor answered by cablegram that the boys were anxious to continue their Nature studies under the tropical sun, but that they were also anxious to spend the coming Christmas at home. As they had collected duplicate material that would far more than pay their expenses, they would like permission to come home for two or three weeks and to return in January. To this Mr. Dawson replied by cablegram, with his usual businesslike brevity: "All well. Come."

This they got soon after they arrived at Constant Spring Hotel, and at once all their spare time was given to getting their collections ready to ship home on the next Atlas Line steamer. In the meantime, the Doctor, who had already the pleasure of acquaintance at King's House, as the residence of Her Majesty Queen Victoria's Governor-General of the island is called, had called on His Excellency the Governor, Sir Henry Arthur Blake and Lady Blake, and on his return had brought with him kindly invitations to the boys to lunch at King's House and inspect the Governor's botanical treasures and Lady Blake's insect collections and miniature menagerie.

King's House stands back from Kingston on the rising plain that reaches from the sea to the mountains and about four miles from the city. When they drove over to it from their hotel, the boys were charmed both by the beauty of its surroundings and the tropical elegance of its arrangement.

The house itself they found to be, like all of those of the wealthy West Indians, planned to keep out hot air and rain in a way that is only possible where cold weather is unknown and stoves and chimneys are unnecessary things. The walls were amply provided with "jalousie" blinds, let into them in panels in such a way as to permit a free play of the air from the spacious porches without allowing one ray of direct sunlight to enter. The polished floors, with here and there a rich rug, and the light, airy furniture combined with the subdued light to give a sense of coolness and repose that was most delightfully refreshing in contrast with the noonday sun outside.

As the Doctor had told them would be the case, they found Sir Henry and Lady Blake what Ned, naturalist-like, afterwards well described as "type specimens of the highest variety of their species"; or, as the Doctor put it, those unsurpassed examples of what the human species is capable of, a true English gentleman and lady. As was natural to young Americans, who had never met any members of the titled English aristocracy, the boys were a little inclined to feel shy at first. But Lady Blake's perfectly prepared collections and equally perfect paintings of the larval and preparatory life of butterflies and moths soon so engrossed their attention that they were entirely at ease and exchanging collecting experiences with Her Ladyship as though they had been lifelong acquaintances.

After luncheon — a thoroughly luxurious, tropical meal — His Excellency, Sir Henry, took his young guests in charge, showing them the wealth of his botanical treasures, his *orchid* collections, rare ferns, and other strange growths, and on their way back to the house exhibited Her Ladyship's pets, a pair of monkeys, a *coatimundi*, or "ant-bear," a full-grown but kitten-like American tiger-cat, quite able to tear one of them to pieces, and some other like rarities. They were so impressed with the charming possibilities of wealth in the tropics, that impulsive Harry declared, much to the amusement of all, that he would never stop teasing until his father had bought a home in Jamaica. Under the care of these entertainers the time soon slipped by, and it was with regret that the boys were compelled finally to listen to the Doctor's admonition about the hour; but an invitation to repeat their visit in the event of their return to the island and then to be members of a party to spend a few days at Sir Henry's lodge in the mountains, a rare collecting field, as Lady Blake's collection proved, reconciled them in a measure.

As they drove away, along the winding roads of the large estate, the great variety of tropical growths, not only native but brought from all warm climates, and the rare insects hovering over this varied collection of bright hues and sweet odors, caused Ned to join Harry in the determination to urge upon their father the beauties and charms of this lovely island as a winter home. Suddenly thinking that where there was so much to charm there must be some decided drawbacks, or else there would be more wealthy men from the bleak North to take advantage of the island's attractions, Ned asked,

"Why don't more Americans come down here, Doctor? They can certainly get here much sooner and more cheaply than they can reach Italy and the south of France, where so many go in winter. Is not the climate just as good; or is there danger of yellow fever here?"

"There is no more native danger of fevers in Kingston than in New York; the few cases of yellow fever that do spring up, perhaps two or three a year, are introduced by sailors and never are allowed to spread. A man of means can have a home in the hills and there he can enjoy for every month in the year a climate such as we have in the delicious days of early June.

"So far as I can see," the Doctor continued, "there is nothing but American ignorance of Jamaica's charms and the fact that it is the fashion to go to the south of France, to Italy, and our own Florida and Southern California, to account for the fact that so few ever taste of this island's sweets. France and Italy have, to be sure, much in the way of antiquity and art to offer, but aside from that neither they nor any part of our country can for an instant compare with Jamaica in climate, in interesting, odd natives, in vegetable luxuriance, or in the wealth of material for research into Nature's ways."

The next day was given to a trip by carriage along the rocky defiles of the Hope River Valley to Gordon Town, and from that point, by an ever climbing trail, on horseback to Newcastle, where the English troops are garrisoned. Well up toward a mile above the sea, high on the rugged slopes of the mountains overlooking Kingston Harbor, far above all danger of fevers or other ills common to the careless dwellers in an army camp, with cosy cottages and gardens for the officers, and comfortable barracks, baths, play-grounds, and a canteen for the men, these English and Irish soldiers lead a more comfortable life there than in most colonial stations. Above them a little way was the dividing ridge of the mountain, and from a gap to which they rode and where they ate their dinner, the boys could clearly see both sides of the island and the blue Caribbean Sea on either hand.

Their homeward way was made lively by an approaching thunder-storm, a thing of almost daily occurrence on these high hills, which chased them down the hillsides as fast as their fleet-footed ponies could go, and finally overtook them with a terrific downpour just as they had reached a sheltering shed by the roadside. Yet, when its fury had passed over and the warm sunshine came back to make everything steam like a hothouse for a few minutes, and they had reached the valley at Gordon Town, they were not a little surprised to find that the road down there was as dry and dusty as it was in the morning. This the Doctor explained by telling them that often during a month or two of drought in the lowlands thunder-storms may be plainly seen every day in the hills.

CHAPTER XV

IN THE HOME OF HOMERUS

Richard, the Driver — The Convicts — Rock Fort — Cane River Falls — The Scarcity of Whites — The Negro Races — The "Gordon Riots" — George William Gordon — The Carnage at Morant Bay — Terrible Retribution — Bath and its Attractions — Cacao, Coca, Coco, and Cocoa — "A *Homerus!* A *Homerus!*" — The Baths of Saint Thomas — A Romantic Legend

THE next day was given up by the boys to the shipment of all their treasures and collections, only their satchels and collecting outfits being retained for the carriage trip to Bath, and on the next morning, when the sun rose out of the Caribbean Sea, they were already several miles on their eastward journey. From Constant Springs to Bath is a distance of forty-eight miles by the road they were to follow, mainly along the southern coast of the island, and if none of the rivers were "down," the Doctor told them, there would be no difficulty in driving the distance in time for a late dinner in the lodging-house in Bath, stopping for an early lunch at Yallah's Bay and taking a hasty peep at some of the sights of the wayside as well.

The rivers on the south coast are treacherous and unmanageable; most of the time they are mere sandy and pebbly gullies, not enough water coming into them from their sources in the hills to reach the sea after all the evaporation and sinking into the parched sands that the hot sun causes, but at other times, when they are turned by the mountain rains into roaring bank-covering torrents, they are quite impassable, and more than one foolhardy traveller has lost his life in attempting to ford them. In his driver the Doctor had implicit confidence, however; for he was known throughout the island as the best in his profession, and even the principal guide-book of the island said of him: "Richard Davis, the best driver in Jamaica, is a perfect guide, and ready reference-book, furnished with marginal notes and bound in brown leather." Richard was everywhere known as the driver who piloted "His 'X'lency, de Gov'nah" around the island, and his knowledge of all the treacherous fordings made the Doctor feel safe in his care.

Three miles east from Kingston, and near the harbor head, the travellers came upon large cliffs from which stone for the macadam roads and for ship ballast is taken by the convicts from the prison near the city. These they saw walking in double file up from the shore, where they had just rowed in barges holding forty or fifty each, and on the back of the light-colored canvas suit of each was painted in large black characters certain cabalistic marks which told their keepers when each had been sentenced, for how long, and the nature of his crime. Just beyond where they were at work was old Rock Fort, once the main fortress and dependence of the Spaniards against English invasion, but long centuries ago abandoned and made useless by the advance in naval warfare. Its blackened, overgrown walls, its buttresses and peep-holes, in one of which a colony of wild bees were busy storing up honey where once the eager Spanish lookout had kept watch, and the roof, long since fallen in, all spoke of days when copper five-pounders and blunderbusses were all that was necessary to guard the rich plains behind them.

The first stop on the road was made when the party came to the Cane River, a rivulet that barely reached the sea, but which Richard told them was of sufficient size about a mile and a half inland to make one of the most striking waterfalls in the West Indies. Leaving their team, they tramped over a winding donkey-path across a mile of hot plains and scrub growth, suddenly coming to a turn in the stream, which oddly increased in size with every yard traversed towards its source, where the rock wall of the hills narrowed in, and a deep gorge had been cut in the mountain by the endless action of the stream. Here the road became a sort of niche cut in the face of the perpendicular precipices, with every now and then a steep grade, so steep in fact that steps had been made that the produce-laden donkeys might gain a firm footing on such steep hills. At the head of the last of these the river, here a stream of some bulk, although no more than would be called a creek in the north, as Harry remarked, bounded over a rocky wall from the pleasant, open valley above, to enter the gorge they had just passed through. Here the road, a public highway and under the care of the parish, passed for several rods through a cave which had undoubtedly at one time been the river's bed. In this cave the boys collected some large centipedes, one of which was eleven inches long and the largest they had ever seen.

During all of this day's drive and during their stop at Yallah's Bay for lunch and at Morant Bay to inspect some of its places of historic interest, the boys were impressed with the absence of white people from the region, and Ned asked the Doctor how the blacks and the half-breeds had got control of everything.

"Perhaps nowhere else on the island have the blacks been given what is called 'full swing' so completely as in this parish of Saint Thomas," was the reply. "No doubt this is to a great extent due to the insurrection of the blacks, known as the 'Gordon Riots,' in 1865, of which I will tell you, but it is also largely due to the fact that it has been less accessible than other regions to steam navigation and therefore less attractive to the white planters. Then, too, for some reason a more determined race of negroes appears to have been introduced to this part of the island in slavery times, and this whole eastern end of the island has displayed a greater degree of self-reliance and intolerance of white rule than the middle or western portions."

"Were the negro races that were brought from Africa so different? I always thought they were all about the same sort," said Harry.

"There were as great differences between them, even greater, perhaps, than now exist in the nations of Europe," the Doctor replied. "The traders brought to the West Indies representatives of almost every tribe on the West Coast of Africa and of its interior for many hundreds of miles. There were Mandingoes, Foulahs, Jolofs, Feletahs, Eboes, Mokos, Congoes, Feloups, Coromantins, Bissagoes,

Shangallas, and others the names of which would be equally new to you. Among these the Mandingoes were noticeable for their temperate habits, enterprise, and cleanliness. They were not black, but a dark brown. They were good accountants, many of them keeping their accounts in the Arabic language. In great contrast to them were the Jolofs, who were jet black, but with regular, almost European features, and of a careless, fiery disposition and opposed to labor. They were the Spaniards of Africa, while the Mandingoes may well be called the English of that continent. The Germans were represented, in turn, by the Foulahs, who were a mild, affable people, fond of hunting, music, and song, and easily governed. They were copper-colored, handsome, tall, slim, with small hands and feet, and thin curved noses. Many students of mankind believe them not to be true Africans, but the descendants from some Eastern people of strong Malay characters, who had come to Africa by way of Madagascar.

"The Eboes were a squat, heavy set, and very black and ugly tribe, tough, careless, cruel, and dissipated; while the Coromantins, like them in color and ugliness, were large, powerful, and very capable men, but much feared by their masters on account of their quarrelsome and incendiary tempers. One sees more Coromantin types of negroes here in Saint Thomas than elsewhere in Jamaica. The Congoes from the coast were a rather intelligent, mild, even-tempered, but lazy, intemperate people, while those of the interior were fierce, dangerous, and murderous cannibals. The Bissagoes were by far the most degraded and beastly, and were excessively superstitious. While these various tribes belonged to the great African stock, they differed very much in appearance, still more in language, and even more in habits and customs. In the latter, however, they were all related by one religious peculiarity, — all were snake-worshippers, or believers in Obeah.

"These facts will enable you to understand why it is that these black people differ so very much and why one man will rise from slavery to the high walks of public life, while those around him stay down in the lower ranks. But the wonder is, nevertheless, that any of them have risen so high and so soon, when we remember how little was done for them until quite recently. During slavery almost nothing was done for their moral instruction; they were allowed to worship snakes to their hearts' content, and only interfered with when their nightly orgies prevented them from doing good work the next day. It is easily within the memory of old persons still living, that a real earnest effort was made to civilize them in the true sense of the term; yet in this island you will find many of them in public places, which they grace and do honor to quite as well as would most of their white neighbors."

At Morant Bay the party halted early in the afternoon to take a look at the town where the "Gordon Riots" had centred. Before 1865 there had been a growing dissatisfaction among the blacks of the island, especially those of this parish, because of the heavy taxes and rents placed on the cultivators of small patches of land, and also because one of these taxes, which was especially heavy, was to support the State Church, of which very few of them were members, but to which all were compelled to contribute, notwithstanding the contributions which they made to their own denominations. Owning several of the finest of these estates, as also some of the best near Kingston, where he lived, was a brown man, George William Gordon, who, although born a slave, had risen to become one of the wealthiest men in the island and a member of its legislature. Gordon had been the slave of his own father, a cold-blooded, selfish white man, who had done little for his son; yet that son's first act when his rare ability won him success as a free man, was to place his heartless father on the very plantation from which the ruin that overwhelmed him on the abolition of slavery had compelled him to move. This was a fair indication of Gordon's goodness of heart, and when it is added to this that he was a very devoutly religious man and very desirous of helping his people, the blacks of the island, to elevate themselves, it is easy to see that he had it in his power to do much good.

Perhaps it was unfortunate that Gordon was an orator, possessed with the power to mould and sway his black hearers even more than he realized; for when he felt called upon to attend their nightly gatherings for worship, and exhort them to stand firm for their rights against the oppression of the whites, his language was so fervent and so full of oratorical flourishes, which he only meant as such, but which they took as advice to them to engage in actual uprisings to arms and bloodshed, that they were beyond his control in a little while. Finally there came a day when certain of their local leaders had been arrested, as they believed unjustly, and the inland hill people came pouring into the town to demand their release and certain reforms, of the parish Council, which was then sitting at the Morant Bay Court House.

Long before they had reached the town, joined on every hand by those living along the way and on the scores of by-ways, the noise of their coming could be heard, the hoarse voices of the men and the shrill cries of the women, — for the women outnumbered the men on that day and far surpassed them in courage and fiendish revenge, — and above all their watch word "Color for color; blood for blood!" called by a thousand ebony throats. White planters on the roads had taken to horse and preceded them to the town to bear the news of their coming, and to seek the protection of the Council and its soldiery. They might quite as well have stayed near their homes and depended on hiding in the bush or in caves; it was only the few whites who did so who lived to tell their side of the story. Their coming only served to inflame and upset the judgment of the parish officers, who at once called out the handful of militia stationed there and barricaded the steps and doors of the town hall.

Having thus shut themselves up in a coop, they seem to have not had sense enough to deny themselves the pleasures of the banquet ordered at the public expense; but when the mob, now numbering its thousands, reached the hall, they were found too busy with the delicacies of the season to give immediate attention to the grievances of such a noisy throng. Even then, had the Custos, or governor of the parish, Baron Ketelholdt, been a man of true courage, he might have averted the terrible result of his cowardly policy of reading the riot act from an upper window, and calling upon the crowds to disperse without giving audience to any of its representatives. These acts were fresh fuel to the flame of their hatred of what they considered white oppression and tyranny, and when in a rash moment the Baron signalled the militia to fire upon the surging mass of blacks, he sealed his own doom and that of all around him.

In those days before the use of repeating rifles, that volley was simply the signal for the multitude to rush in upon the soldiers, with their discharged guns, and hack them to pieces with cutlasses and pruning-hooks, or batter them into shapeless masses with clubs and axe-helves. While one small portion of the mob was thus engaged, another set fire to the town hall, in which was caged every white man in the place, while a still larger portion set out through the town, bent on burning or looting every bit of property belonging to a white, and killing every man, woman, and child of that color encountered. Roasted out of the pen of their own choosing, the Custos and his followers simply escaped from the wrath of the flames to the worse torments of the furies below.

Then was awakened all the slumbering ferocity of the savage African ancestry. Not content with wreaking vengeance on those who were the immediate cause of their troubles, the blacks spread throughout the whole parish, and for several days scoured the country in search of every white person, or of any mulatto who was suspected of secret sympathy with the whites. Killing and burning, pillaging and wanton destruction, ruled for several days, until the frightened authorities at Kingston had sufficiently gathered their wits together to send troops and marines to the rescue of this wretched neighborhood. But even then the bloodshed and inexcusable murder were far from arrested; for the tables were simply turned, and the troops only reproduced the atrocities of the blacks by visiting their vengeance on hundreds of unoffending, ignorant people.

Gordon was sent for and brought to Morant Bay from Kingston in irons, hastily tried by a court-martial, without the due formalities of law, given no chance to prove his innocence of inciting riots by which he was one of the greatest sufferers, found guilty, and hung where his body could be seen for several days by his one-time followers, and then cut down to be buried in a compost heap, it is said. Such were the "Gordon Riots," as they have been unjustly called. It is small wonder that dark and savage looks on black faces and but few whites to be seen anywhere have long been the characteristics of the parish. But all that is now changed. Where once there were half-starved blacks there are now an abundance of thrifty growers of fruit, and the black man who cannot now live in a manner very comfortable to him, and have a little savings account as well, has no one but himself to blame. For the banana, cacao, cocoanut, and nutmeg crops have sprung up into such activity that the small planter is now quite independent of the uncertainties of the large sugar and rum estates.

While these interesting scraps of history were being told them with a wealth of illustration in the very localities where so many of the occurrences took place, the boys had been bowling along over a hard, macadamized road through a country crowded with vegetable luxuriance and variety. The road in most places was embowered in the dense growths of bamboo, silk-cotton, and mango trees, and, as the fast-falling twilight came on, their way became more and more lost in the shadows. While Richard drove on at as rapid a gait as ever, secure in the knowledge of the always excellent condition of the road, the boys showed increasing signs of nervousness, now and then glancing from side to side as they passed through some specially dark spot, until the Doctor remarked with a laugh,

"You young men need have no fears, I can assure you. The days of 1865 are only shadowy memories now, and there is no place on the earth where I could possibly feel more secure in spending my days than here about Bath. Isn't it a very peaceful place now, Richard?"

"'Deed it is, Mastah Doctor!" replied their usually taciturn driver. "Day ain't no needs o' fear roun' dis part o' de lan' now-days. Mens is too hard a'wok makin' money in de b'nana walks fer to tink o' de bad times o' ole Gordon."

There was hardly need for this speech, a rather extensive one for Richard, for it was barely finished before they had forded the Plantain Garden River and, driving up the long single street of Bath, had pulled up before the cheerful-looking house of Mistress Duffy, the landlady of the town. The Doctor was soon recognized; and the greetings were pleasant,—for Bath had once been his headquarters on a collecting tour,—and in a little while they were ushered into a dining-room where the table was crowded with all the good things of the neighborhood.

Realizing that their time was very limited, and that on their return to the island they would have more time for general collecting, Ned and Harry decided to make the old Botanical Garden, a rich treasure house of rare trees and plants, the Baths of Saint Thomas the Apostle up the valley of the Sulphur River, and the hunting for *Papilio Homerus*, one of the world's rarest butterflies, the three important items of this visit. In the Botanical Garden, now no longer under cultivation, other than keeping out weeds and the wild undergrowth, they found many plants and trees new to them. The camphor tree, several rare palms, the cork tree, rattans, the India rubber tree, and many small curiosities were among the number shown to them, and from each they were allowed to make generous collections for their herbarium.

All the botanical treasures of the region were not in this garden, however; for the grounds of a former botanist in charge of the garden, now dead, were inspected by them under the guidance of his widowed daughter, who added to her father's love for plants the entomologist's zeal, and exhibited to them some of her rarer captures, among which were many things that made the boys' eager eyes dance with delight at the thought that they too might add the same to their trophies. Various kinds of fibre plants were here growing, and nutmegs, jack-fruit,

Otaheite pears, and cacao, or chocolate-berry, were among the things newest to their inspection.

"Doctor, we always say 'cocoa' in the north, but you and all these people where it grows say 'cacao,' I notice. How is that?" asked Hal.

"There are four very distinct vegetable growths that have names so much alike that they are constantly mixed in the minds of those who are not botanists or do not know them in nature," the Doctor began. "These are: Cacao berries, Coca leaves, Coco roots, and Cocoa nuts. Much as these names resemble each other, they represent four families in the plant world as dissimilar as are apples, huckleberries, lilies, and pine trees. Yet it is the fact that very many, perhaps most people, in northern countries believe them all to be derived from one growth, the cocoa-nut palm, and even our leading dictionaries get them badly mixed.

"Cacao, or chocolate berries, grow on this short tree, not unlike a big lilac bush, to which Linneus gave the very appropriate name, *Theobroma cacao*, the first part of it meaning 'food for the gods,' and the latter being derived from the Mexican or Aztec 'cacauatl,' their word for chocolate. The word should be pronounced as though spelled *kah-cow'*, with the accent on the last syllable. From this tree we get the chocolate, cocoa, broma, cocoa-butter and cocoa-shells sold in the north.

"Coca leaves grow on an Andean bush much like our mountain huckleberries, and called *Erythroxolon coca*, and are largely used by the Inca natives to stimulate and strengthen them for feats of endurance. A few of the dried leaves will, as I have myself found, enable one to walk all day over the tedious mountain trails, covering perhaps thirty or more miles without a morsel of other food. From them is made the wine of coca, now so common in northern drug stores; and 'moxie,' a stimulating drink, named after a naval lieutenant, is also derived from it. Cocaine, now much used in surgery to deaden pain, is also a product of this useful plant. The word is to be pronounced *koh-kah'*, with the accent on the last syllable.

"Coco, pronounced *koh-koh*, with the accent equal on each syllable, is a name representing several eatable roots of certain lily-like plants, that are useful in supplying tubers where potatoes and mandioca roots are not to be had. They are not sent to the north, but are grown somewhat in the hills of this island.

"Cocoanuts are the best known in their natural state of any of the four families of plants we have been discussing. As you already well know, they are the product of the palm tree which has so often yielded us the delights of its luscious nuts and of the great value of which to all tropic-dwelling natives we have already talked. The tree is named *Cocos nucifera*, and the word cocoa should be pronounced *koh'-kwah*, with the accent on the first syllable."

While the boys were at lunch that day, discussing a trip up the Sulphur River for the afternoon, Ned suddenly sprang from the table with a bound, exclaiming,

"Oh! what a beauty! Doctor, Doctor! what is that magnificent creature?" meanwhile pointing out of the window to a nearby rosebush in full bloom, over which was hovering by far the most superb butterfly they had yet seen. Lazily flitting from rose to rose, its nearly seven inches of broad, velvety black expanse, banded with a great golden dash across both wings, with golden fringings and blue and purple eyelike spots on the hind wings, it presented in the glistening sunlight an appearance that was never to be forgotten. Usually the Doctor was an interested but entirely calm observer of their very natural enthusiasm, but in this instance their zeal was infectious; for he rushed into the adjoining room and out of the house, with his net in his hand, calling:—

"A *Homerus!* A *Homerus!* One like that is worth fifty dollars; besides being a great credit to the one who can capture it."

Quickly the boys followed, and as Mistress Duffy, with a smile, put away the eatables that they had so suddenly forgotten, knowing well that that was the last she would see of them for some time, she wisely shook her head and muttered something about the boys being just as crazy as the Doctor.

It is one thing to see a *Homerus* hovering over flower-laden bushes, and quite another to capture it; for they are as shy of man and as powerful of wings as most birds. So the boys found it in this case; for no sooner had they reached the garden than the glorious creature rapidly sailed away over the tree-tops in a direction that the Doctor said would soon bring it to the Sulphur River valley, towards which they at once started on a rapid walk by a roundabout, but good road. In their eagerness to overtake the coveted prize, the boys did not take note that they were walking along a beautiful, shaded valley with high-growing hills on both sides, along a good carriage-road, with every now and again a shed across the roadway, under which to drive in case of a tropical downpour of rain; but all their eagerness availed them nothing, and they had reached the bath-house before they gave up all hope of again seeing it.

The bath-house they found to be a neatly built and well-kept, two-story building, with five private bathrooms, for the use of which a shilling was charged. Each of these rooms had a concrete tank in the floor, about three feet deep and wide and seven feet long, with arrangement for turning streams of cold or hot sulphur water from springs further up the stream into it. By this means a bath varying from 70 to 125 degrees in temperature could be taken, and the water could be gradually changed while the bath was being enjoyed. The waters were known to be very beneficial for rheumatism, gout, and certain skin diseases, and the old man and his wife who took care of the place were full of accounts of the good it had done for many patients, many of whom had come there and lived in the rooms above the baths, and of legends regarding the early history of the baths. The account of how they had been first discovered, although probably nothing but legend, so interested the boys that Ned wrote it in his notebook to use in his next letter home.

In the early years of the English occupancy of the island, perhaps two hundred years ago, a slave had escaped from one of the lowland plantations near the coast and found a secure hiding-place in the mountains. The poor fellow was much troubled with the yaws, a sort of leprous skin disease, and in fact was so far gone with the disorder that his master did not think it worth while to chase him and recapture him. Some year or more after this another planter lost a slave in these mountains, and on returning from a trip during which the runaway was captured, he told the other that he had seen but failed to capture the first runaway, who had grown to be, strange to relate, a fine, healthy man again. Of course healthy slaves were too valuable to lose in this way, and the owner set after him, and in time succeeded in capturing him, when he was found to be thoroughly cured of the yaws and in perfect health.

When pressed for an explanation of his remarkable recovery from a disease, then believed to be incurable, he remained silent or would only give misleading replies. The owner had a much-loved daughter who had an equally incurable and terrible trouble of the same nature, and in his desire to have her share the benefits of such a miraculous cure, he finally offered freedom to the slave if he would disclose the source of his recovery. When the effect of the healing waters that poured into the Sulphur River from a number of springs was explained to him, he was not long in arranging to have a cottage erected there, to be under the charge of his freed slave, in which his daughter and her attendants could live; and she in time became the first white of a long line of sufferers who have learned to bless the waters of the Baths of Saint Thomas the Apostle.

CHAPTER XVI

A MIDNIGHT HORROR

Hunting *Homerus* — Loathsome Bait — A Profitable Day — Cuna Cuna Pass — Ideal Roads — The Maroons — A Barbarous Execution — A Deserting Guide — Blood-curdling Sounds — A Lost Burro — The Valley of the Rio Grande — Wholesale Fruit Culture

THE remainder of the time at Bath was spent in the endeavor, by various devices, to induce a few of the specimens of *Papilio Homerus*, which every now and then they saw sailing idly over head, to come within reach of their nets. Cocoanut palms and other trees that were laden with sweet-scented flowers from climbing vines were ascended, and in two of the most promising localities platforms, such as they had made in Haiti, were constructed in tall trees, but beyond three rather imperfect specimens they had nothing to show for such toilsome methods. Another plan, however, proved much more effective. On their first day at Bath the Doctor had brought a salt codfish, and after shredding it apart, had placed it on a board in the sun to spoil, covering it with a piece of wire screen so that the buzzards would not touch it, and placing it near enough to a chained watch dog to prevent ground animals from getting at it. Three days afterwards, when this fish was getting "pretty rank," as Ned termed it, the Doctor boiled it in about five gallons of water until the result was a thickish, ill-smelling fluid.

This mess they carried up the Sulphur River to a point some distance above the baths, where the stream widened out and a bridle path crossed it. There on several flat stones, slightly hollowed out on top, they poured the liquid in the bright sunlight, as well as on two open spaces in the road. This they did early in the morning, returning to take a bath at the springs and then to their boarding-house for lunch. After lunch they returned to the bait, hardly believing that so repulsive a broth could attract such gorgeous creatures as the regal *Homerus*, although the Doctor reminded them of how often they had caught choice specimens at home around filthy mud puddles or near the stable yard. As they advanced cautiously from out of the shade into the open space where were the baited stones, the boys' hearts almost stood still at seeing three apparently perfect specimens of this most coveted prize quietly sipping away in the centre of a group of at least fifty other butterflies of perhaps a dozen different species.

"Gently, gently!" the Doctor cautioned. "*Homerus* will not take fright quickly, but some of those little blue beauties on the outside of the group will, and the moment they begin to fly up the whole group will take fright, and instantly *Homerus* will be far over the tree-tops. Let us come up slowly and equally from each side; then the moment they begin to rise, Ned must bring his net down over the group so as to catch all three, if possible, while Harry and I will try to capture what escape him, on the wing."

This plan, well laid as it seemed, resulted in the cap-

ture of only one specimen, however; for the two that
escaped Ned's net were too quick for his reinforcements,
as well. But the one taken was so superb a creature and
the other specimens captured in the frantic efforts to let
nothing escape were some of them such valuable additions
to their collections, that the day would have then been
voted a very productive one, without even greater success
at another of the rocks and still better fortune in the road,
where five of the *Homerus* species, three of which they
captured, awaited them. This was indeed a wonderful
afternoon's exploit; and the Doctor cautioned the boys
against taking it as a sample of what was ordinarily
possible. They had simply been fortunate in reaching
Bath at the height of the *Homerus* season, and in a very
good season at that. The number they would take away
perhaps equalled all that had ever been taken in one year
before. He had spent weeks there before, and had not
even seen so many.

"Is *Homerus* found in many other countries, Doctor?"
Harry asked, as they walked home. "Is it found all
over this island?"

"No, to both of those questions," was the reply. "It
has been seen in Haiti by one collector, but otherwise it is
unknown outside of Jamaica, so far as known to naturalists. Nor has it often been seen far away from this part
of the island. In fact, it is safe to say that it belongs
naturally in or near the valley of the Sulphur River, and
in the mountains around or above it. What this is due to,
no one has yet attempted to explain. It would seem that so
large a species and one so powerful on the wing ought to be

wide-spread throughout this island at least, even if it did not also indulge in migrations from one island to another; but such is not the case, for it is one of the most geographically narrow species in its distribution known to science."

A day or two after this great triumph over the difficulties incident to capturing *Homerus* saw the boys by daybreak already some distance on their way towards crossing the Blue Mountains at Cuna Cuna Pass, one of the most beautiful gaps in the great range which divides the island lengthwise into two nearly equal halves. To make this trip it was necessary to resort again to travel in the saddle, as they had done in Haiti, and to send their large baggage around by the stage road to Port Antonio, their destination, and the point from which they were soon to start for their northern home.

The climb up and over these mountains served more than ever to impress the boys with the vast difference that exists between witchcraft-cursed Haiti and freedom-blessed Jamaica. Where, in Haiti, the mountain views looked out only on wildernesses and desolation, although the fertility and climate were unexcelled, in Jamaica every view added new charms to the scene, and these charms were greatly added to by the varied views of cultivation; bananas here and cane-fields there, cocoanut groves on one hand and cacao or coffee on the other. Even the road they travelled, although it crossed steep mountains over a winding route, spoke for the excellence of the way affairs are administered under Her Majesty's Government, even in such small items as the mountain bridle paths in one of the smaller colonies.

"Why is it that down here, in a blackman's country, they can have so much better country roads than we do in the United States?" Ned asked, as they were starting down the northern slope of the mountains.

"Simply because it appears to have been reserved for us at home to imagine that politics had anything to do with such primary necessities as good roads, good streets, good water, and good health. We have a way in the States of considering a man's politics first and his fitness for his work last, even in such minor places as that of road commissioner; therefore the man elected thinks far more of working to keep the political party that gave him his job in good order than he does of giving his attention to keeping the roads in good order. Here they know nothing of politics in that sense, and a road boss is judged simply by the sort of roads he maintains. The great difference between the systems is that ours gives us mud-puddles and deep ruts in place of the hard, even surfaces we find here, although we have nothing like the enormous rainfall to contend with that they have here."

Having found a good camping-spot early in the afternoon, the mules were unloaded and tethered, and the rest of the day was given to collecting. While this was going on, the Doctor explained to the boys that they were now in Maroon territory, or a land commonly claimed by the mountain Maroons. To Harry's query as to who and what the Maroons were, he replied that the name was derived from the Spanish word *cimarron*, a wild man, and was originally applied in Columbus's time to those Indians who had been enslaved, but had escaped to the mountains or wildernesses and had successfully defended themselves against recapture. When the Indian slaves were nearly all killed off by Spanish cruelty, and Africans were introduced in their places, these in many cases also escaped and joined the small Indian settlements in the wild regions, and in this way there grew up here and there, scattered throughout the West Indies, wherever the difficulty of access made it hard for the whites to penetrate, small communities of half-savages. In Jamaica these thrived in the genial mountain climate and rapidly grew to be a numerous and formidable people.

From time to time, for over two hundred years, the white planters in the lowlands organized expeditions to recapture and enslave these people, who from time to time retaliated, making sudden forays into the lowlands, when there was much bloodshed and pillaging, and many other slaves were forcibly liberated to join them. In the early part of the last century this warfare was almost constant, lasting for nearly forty years, and it was not until many concessions, such as the grants of land and the recognition of their rights as free men had been made them, that the Maroons agreed to a peace based on a regular treaty made between them and Governor Trelawney. During the time before the treaty these valleys and mountain sides were the scenes of many fearful conflicts between the white troops and the Maroons under the leadership of a chief named Nanny. This man was a fearless and able leader, and tradition has it that only through the treachery of one of his people was it possible for the troops to gain access to his stronghold on a high bluff overlooking the

Stony river. Here when they were surrounded by superior numbers and overpowered by superior arms, these brave strugglers after freedom preferred to cast themselves over the bluffs, choosing sudden death on the rocks beneath rather than the slow torture of slavery.

Nanny, however, the tradition states, was wounded early in the battle and in that condition was loaded with chains and hung from the top of the bluff in plain sight for miles around as a warning to the poor blacks who dared to fight for freedom. There he was left to die a slow death, parched by the sun and tortured by the buzzards by day, and numbed by the mountain air and buffeted by the bats by night. Legend has it that slowly and little by little this terrible sight disappeared until even the last links of the chain had rusted away and fallen to the ravine below. In after years there began to come rumors, from men who had been belated in the bear chase on these mountains, of terrible sights and sounds, which finally took the shape of an indescribable form wandering along in the moonlight, dragging a great length of clanking chain after it. From time to time some one who had ventured into these higher hills failed to return, and as these were usually white men, it became a generally accepted theory that Nanny in the spirit walked again through his old domain and would not brook the intrusion of any white therein. To-day there are very many of the blacks hereabouts who cannot be in any way induced to stay over night on these mountains, and even the most intelligent of them while passing over the mountains have a wonderful ingenuity in finding good excuses for passing the night in the settled valleys below.

As though specially to support this last assertion on the Doctor's part, their guide and muleteer hunted them up just then, and, stating that he had fed and cared for two of the mules and made a good fire, asked to be allowed to take the other mule and spend the night with a brother who lived about six miles down the road. Winking at the boys, the Doctor at first refused the request, but as the seriousness of his predicament finally drove the man into a network of falsehoods, he at last gave his consent, a grant that was taken advantage of so eagerly and so immediately as to be ludicrous. They found a good fire awaiting them, and it was not long before one of them got an appetizing meal ready while the others were busied in erecting the tent and fixing camp for the night.

Such days as these, full of events and of toil, make long nights and early bed-going welcome, and the cool, crisp mountain air makes sleep an easy task. How long they had all been asleep when Ned woke up to tuck his blanket more closely around him he did not know, nor is it likely he would ever have cared to know had he not, just as he was about to doze off again, been startled into the widest kind of wakefulness by a most peculiar sound, not very far off. He knew it could not be either of their mules; for they had been tethered some distance from them where there was an open spot suitable for grazing, too far away for him to hear their movements; yet this sound was very near at hand. First a swishing sound as of some moving creature passing along a clump of bushes, then a footfall, then a painfully long period of silence and suspense, then another sound, as of a chain dragged along the ground.

Perhaps if it had not been for that last sound Ned might have fallen asleep again, for he was most wofully tired; but just then he thought of that headless, shapeless thing which was said to consider the mountain slopes his own and resent in deadly fashion the intrusion of any daring white who thought to challenge his authority. Ned was not a coward, nor did he believe in anything ghostly; yet in spite of all he felt his blood running cold, and a paralyzing shiver taking hold of him as again he heard those sounds, and now much nearer.

There could be no mistaking them; the stealthy, muffled tread, the peculiar swish of the bushes pushed aside, a sighing sound as of one near at hand trying to stifle heavy breathing, and — far worse and more suggestive than all — that clanking chain. Then again followed a long period of silence — harder to bear than the fear-begetting sounds. Just as Ned was getting his pistol in a position to greet any sudden apparition and preparing to slip quietly from the bed with the intention of peeping out into the open air, however terrible the form or nature of the intruder, every drop of blood in his veins seemed frozen, every iota of bravery in his heart was put to flight, by a succession of sounds that were unequalled in their appalling volume.

"EE-haw, ee-haw, ee-haw; yah-yah-yah-yah!"

Startled beyond control of his actions, the first unmistakable asinine bray was the signal for the firing of Ned's pistol, a deafening sound that brought the Doctor and Harry to their feet under the impression that they were the victims of a murderous onslaught from the always peaceful natives. Fright and consternation, however, soon had to give way to peals of laughter when Ned had explained to his companions the terrible mental strain through which he had just gone and the nature of the sounds that caused it. If the spirit of the old Maroon chieftain still haunts those mountains, he must have paused in outraged wonder to hear their shouts of merriment as, time after time, the utter ludicrousness of the whole thing impressed them anew.

But if they had at first been badly frightened, they had not been alone in that respect. Long after their laughter had subsided, far down the mountain side, sounding quite two miles away, came back, in tones much mellowed by the distance, the same refrain, "Ee-haw, ee-haw," that before had petrified Ned in horror. Evidently the four-footed intruder, much demoralized by his noisy reception, had been doing some pretty rapid travelling since he had attempted to fill the role of evil spirit. And the next morning, as they journeyed down the mountains towards Moore Town, a Maroon village, they were met by an old blackman, who, after a deferential bow, remarked,

"Mawnin', buckra, mawnin', young genmen! Yo' yain't none o' yo' seen nuthin' o' no jackass, is yo? No jackass wiv a chain a' hangin' to him? Kase, ef yo' has an' yo' has hearn him blow him bugle, yo'se boun' to know it. I'se los' a Jack what's got a trumpet dat'll out-blow de las' horn!"

Assured that they had not seen his property, but that they felt pretty sure that he had visited them during the night, the old man trudged joyfully upward, glad to know that he was on the right track.

Moore Town and the occasional gatherings of huts along the way to the lower valley of the Rio Grande (Grand River) and their inhabitants appeared so exactly like other Jamaican huts and natives that the boys had seen, that the Doctor had to explain that the Maroons had for so long intermarried with the other negroes that it was impossible to tell them from the rest. If the boys expected to find them still semi-savage, they were doomed to disappointment, for there is nowhere in the island a more loyal and law-abiding portion of its people than the Maroons are now. It was largely due to their aid that the Gordon Riots of 1865 were so quickly overcome; for they had, in accordance with their first treaty with the authorities, always quickly responded to such a call as that.

As the party reached the lower and widened valley of the Rio Grande, now grown to considerable size from the additions of several large streams, the country took on a much less wild and uncultivated aspect, for they were entering upon one of the choicest parts of the island for banana cultivation. Here at Golden Vale, they found large plantations in a most thriving condition belonging to a northern corporation, which operated many large estates in the island, and ran a fleet of their own steamers between Jamaica and Boston, laden with bananas, cocoanuts, oranges, limes, pineapples, and early vegetables. Under the guidance of "Busher" Davis, a jolly man, whose arduous duties of managing this large estate seemed to be mere pleasure to him, all the details of banana culture were explained to the boys. How the plants were set out as slips or rootlets, for bananas have no seeds, and grew to varying heights, from ten to eighteen feet and bore a bunch of bananas in from seven to ten months; how when about a month from being ripe, the bunch was cut down and the stalk on which it grew was also cut down, the broad leaves to be used in wrapping the bunches, and the big, fleshy stalk to be left on the ground as enrichment; and how carefully the bunches were handled in large, haywagon-like carts and sent to Port Antonio, five miles away, was all made plain to them. There was much to see at Golden Vale, which with all its dependencies contained 3500 acres of rich and blossoming land, but the news that a steamer was even then loading at the Port, on which they could take passage to Philadelphia, warned them that time was too precious to be even so pleasantly spent.

The rest of their way to Port Antonio was along a garden spot throughout, bordered by plantations large and small, everything giving proof of a degree of enterprise and thrift quite unknown until the banana cultivation was introduced. Everywhere were jolly, contented faces, and everywhere were signs that more land was being pressed into the service of the far-away, hungry northland.

It was dark when the boys arrived at Port Antonio, and as their steamer expected to leave port as soon as loaded, probably before daybreak, they had but little chance to see anything of the town and its four or five thousand inhabitants, for their time was mainly taken up with getting their belongings on board.

CHAPTER XVII

BACK TO THE FROZEN NORTH

Deceptive Clouds — A Comprehensive View — From Straw Hats to Ulsters — A Glad Home-coming — Mr. Dawson's Plans — The Doctor's Words of Praise — The Work at the Academy — A Proud Moment — A Well-earned Honor — A Handsome Balance — "Ho! for the Spanish Main!"

WHEN the boys awoke the next morning, the churning of the propeller and the motion of the ship told them that they had left Jamaica during the night, and they hurried on deck to catch a last glimpse of the beautiful island. The varied labors of the previous day had made late rising easy, and they found that they had not come on deck one bit too soon, for the hazy outlines of the mountains on which they had been camped only twenty-four hours before were barely discernible on the southern horizon in a faint streak that was quite as much like a bank of clouds as a real mountain range.

"It's hard to tell the difference between those Blue Mountains to the right, and that bank of clouds to the left," said Harry, as they stood looking astern.

"Yes," the Doctor remarked, "for the very simple reason that what you call 'the bank of clouds to the left' is in reality the southwestern spur of Haiti, which we bade good-bye to a few days ago."

"Is that so? Why, I had no idea that we could see Jamaica and Haiti at the same time," said Harry. "But, anyhow, I was right about it being hard to tell mountains from clouds at such a distance, for in this other direction there seem to be the same sort of ranges," he added, turning towards the north.

"True enough," the Doctor said, laughing, "and again for the very simple reason that those are the mountains that skirt the south shore of the eastern end of Cuba. For, you see, we now happen to be just about equidistant from each of the islands, and each of them has a mountain range sufficiently high to be seen at this distance when the atmosphere is so beautifully clear as it is this morning. You were right, however, Hal, in saying that clouds and mountains appear precisely alike at a great distance, as no doubt you will observe as we go up the coast of the United States, where often there will appear to be large and imposing ranges where only low sand dunes and low swamps are found. There are some old sailors who will assure you that they can always tell 'the loom of the land,' as they call it, from the deceptive appearance of clouds, but for my part I am very doubtful about their possessing such skill."

The trip northward was an uneventful one. The frowning sides of Cape Maisi, at the eastern point of Cuba, were all that was new to them; the passage up the Bahamas being through the region where their first tastes of tropical life were derived, and the rest of the voyage being out of sight of land until the low shores of Delaware and New Jersey were discerned bordering the smoother waters of the Delaware Bay. The boys had become better sailors, and the sea was unusually smooth, and not one hour was lost from the work of assorting and arranging collections, putting the finishing touches on their diaries, and writing a number of letters, about the extra material they would have to dispose of, to be mailed on landing to certain museums and private collectors with whom the Doctor was acquainted. The only unpleasant or at all striking fact observable on the northward trip was due to the rapid fall in the temperature. The boys left Port Antonio in the lightest of summer clothing and under straw hats; after successive changes of under- and over-clothing, they reached Philadelphia in the heaviest of winter clothes, unable to get well warmed even in their storm coats, to find the ground white with snow and the river filled with ice through which a passage had constantly to be cleared by the powerful rams of the ice-boats.

Cold as was the weather, it was all forgotten in the joyous warmth of the greeting that awaited the boys at the wharf. It was almost Christmas time, and the usual holiday shopping had brought Mrs. Dawson and her daughter to the city, so that it was the entire family — father, mother, and their three children — who eagerly talked very fast and merrily together, perhaps to hide the least suspicion of moisture in the eyes and trembling of the voices, so glad was the reunion. Nor was the all-careful guardian, Dr. Bartlett, forgotten in the rejoicing; for among the first plans made after he had been cordially thanked by both Mr. and Mrs. Dawson for his watchful care of their boys, Mr. Dawson made this anouncement:—

"We shall stay in the city until the day before Christmas, Doctor, and Mrs. Dawson and I shall expect you to be our guest at the hotel. I have seen the curators at the Academy of Natural Sciences, and they have very kindly put a room at your disposal, for the unpacking and assorting of the material you have brought back. There you and the boys can do your work to the best advantage, no doubt getting much aid and many suggestions from the professors of the Academy, and I have decided to buy of you one set or series of your collections, such as the curators may select, which we will present to the Academy in the name of the boys. You will, of course, spend Christmas with us, Doctor, just as one of the family, and after the holidays are over you and the boys can return for a while to this city to continue your arrangements for dividing and selling your duplicate material."

"I am very much indebted to you and Mrs. Dawson for your kind invitation, I assure you," the Doctor replied. "As I have, as you know, nowhere to go among relatives, I shall accept it with pleasure and gratitude. The arrangements made by you are most excellent, for the superior library and large collections of the Academy will be most helpful to us, and we shall need all the help we can get, if we are to return to our explorations in the West Indies before February first, as we hope to do."

"There is only one condition, you will remember, that I made as to your return," said Mr. Dawson, now addressing the boys as well. "And that is that before I give my consent to your return you must be able to show me by the results of this trip, that your second trip will be self-supporting. By this I simply mean that I make you boys a present of all your expenses on this trip, but before I shall be willing to advance you the money for the next one, I shall want a report from the Doctor, telling me that your saleable material will in time bring in enough to enable you to repay me for the advance. Of course, I am quite able to send you out as often as you want to go or as often as your mother and I think it best for you to be away from us; but we both think it will be a good business training, and always a pleasant memory for you to be able to say that these vacation expeditions were altogether self-supporting. If that is so, I now see no reason why the Doctor should not take you back to Jamaica about February first, and from there take you to the Central American mainland for a three months' trip. If after that you want to spend another three or four months in northern South America, providing your collection has been a success, and we are all in perfect health, I see no reason at present why you should not do so. I have just heard that your school has been closed permanently, and it will not be advisable to enter you now in another school until next fall's term. Besides that, I am quite certain that the sort of practical schooling that you are now getting under the Doctor's care, is the very best for you just now, and a year thus spent in the school of Nature cannot help being very beneficial to you."

This was a very long speech for the usually quiet and taciturn Mr. Dawson, more a man of affairs than of words, but it was one that filled the boys with delight, and impulsive Hal eagerly replied,

"Oh! then we are sure to go! Why, Doctor, those *Papilios* that we took in the tree-top at Laguna Enriquillo and the *Papilio Homerus* catch at Bath will bring enough to send us out again, won't they?"

"Well, perhaps hardly that," was the Doctor's cautious but smiling reply; "they will certainly go a great way towards it, and with the great wealth of other butterflies, all the beetles and other insects, and the birds, snakes, fishes, and smaller alcoholic collections we have to unpack, I feel sure that we shall not only have the assurance of funds for another trip, but also quite a handsome little balance to our credit.

"I hardly think," the Doctor continued, turning to Mr. Dawson, "that you realize how industrious these young men have been, and how steadily they have adhered to the one purpose of bringing back collections thoroughly representative of the region in which they have been travelling. I feel quite safe in saying that no expedition that has visited those islands, composed of only three collectors and in the field so short a time, has done better. I am certain that after years of experience as a collector, I can truthfully say that I have never had such ardent and energetic assistants before. You will be surprised when you see the entire results of our little expedition displayed; you cannot yet form an idea of how extensive it really is."

"I imagine that I have some idea of its bulk at least," Mr. Dawson said laughingly; "for I have had notification from the Custom House authorities, that boxes, barrels, crates, and bundles, weighing in all 7650 pounds, are waiting our orders at the wharves. Over three and a half tons of butterflies and bugs, snakes and lizards, sounds pretty big to me; although I am hardly yet prepared to look upon such things as regular merchandise, saleable in the market like iron, or lumber, or cloth goods. But I hope your impressions of their worth may be found correct; this is your trade, Doctor, and when you tell me, after going over it all, that the material for sale, after keeping out a full set for the boys' museum at home, will bring as much as your trip just finished has cost, I shall be sure you are right, and quite as well pleased with the result as the boys themselves."

The next few days were spent in getting the many packages from the wharves to the Academy and in unpacking them and getting the various sorts of collections together, ready for the final sorting. After the Christmas and New Year's holidays were over, — holidays that were all the more joyous for the boys because of their previous absence from home, — the Doctor and the boys returned to Philadelphia and set to work at the more careful arrangement of their trophies. Doctor Bartlett, well acquainted with this work, knowing how much time was taken up in attaching labels to each separate specimen from the smaller boxes, on which one label was sufficient while they were all kept together before being arranged in different series, engaged a typewriter clerk to keep up with this work. And for the simple arranging of the various classes and order he employed two of the students at the Academy to help the boys in extra hours, while in the more difficult arrangement and separation of one species of a family from another he was greatly aided by some of the professors, all specialists and experts in different fields of Nature, who were glad to do such work, knowing that a choice series of the collections was to be presented to their institution. Thus excellent progress was made.

As, day by day, their trophies of the chase, their gatherings of many days and nights of almost ceaseless watchfulness, were spread out and arrayed, the boys grew more and more surprised at the bulk of the work they had really accomplished. Doctor Bartlett was the only one who from the very first had an accurate idea of just how much they had brought back with them. As the collections grew in importance each day, and the professors saw how excellently the boys had done in the field chosen by them, it was agreed that the Academy should give them a reception, inviting all its members and their friends to be present some evening to inspect a display of their collections and to meet the young collectors. Of course, to this great event, Mr. and Mrs. Dawson, their sister, and some friends at home were invited, and it was a proud moment for the two nervous, blushing boys when they stood by the side of the grave old President of the Academy and were introduced in a few well-chosen remarks.

"This institution, ladies and gentlemen," the President began, "has in time past welcomed to its hospitalities many renowned discoverers and explorers. When I mention such names as Kane, Peary, and Heilprin of Arctic fame, Stanley, Du Chaillu, Abbot, and Peters of African renown, Huxley, Tindall, Ball, Von Siebold, and many others in the world of research, it will be appreciated how highly honored these halls have been in time past by the presence of men now and then renowned. To night it is my pleasure to introduce to you two young men who are remarkable among all the long line of honored guests in being by far the youngest of the array. They may be youthful Huxleys or Von Siebolds, their philosophical powers yet in hiding, but they cannot be said to have been keeping their powers of endurance and painstaking observation of Nature and her ways in hiding, as the very large and complete display of their abilities in that respect, now about us on every hand, amply testifies. It adds a double zest to our pleasure in inspecting these treasures of the Indies to learn that it is their generous intention to donate a complete set of them to this institution, and it will, no doubt, afford all an equal pleasure to know that the Academy has decided to confer upon them the distinction of Corresponding Membership, in return both for their generosity and in recognition of their contributions to science in bringing back for our study a number of forms of animal life entirely new to the naturalists. I therefore have much pleasure in introducing to you the guests of the evening, our youngest members, Edward Randolph Dawson and Henry Murray Dawson."

This speech was greeted with a buzz of applause and a number of cries of "Speech, speech!" during which Ned and Hal looked at each other most uncomfortably, appalled at the thought that one of them must make a few remarks in reply to the honor conferred upon them. After a short but rather awkward pause, Ned advanced to the edge of the platform and said in as steady a voice as he could command,

"My brother and I are very thankful for the great honor done us to-night. If we have added rare things to the collections here, we are very glad of it. At any rate, the credit belongs more to our friend and instructor, Doctor Bartlett, who knew just where to take us and told us all we know about Natural History collecting."

Then the Doctor was called on for a speech, the President in introducing him stating that he had not been honored by a membership then because for years he had been an active member of the Academy, and the Doctor replying in a few words bearing witness to the eagerness and thoroughness of his young companions on the expedition. All this was very gratifying to the boys' parents, and, as their father congratulated them afterwards, he added,

"Never mind about the profits of the trip; I guess after to-night I can send you on another whatever they are."

"Oh, they are assured now, as this report shows," the Doctor broke in, as he handed Mr. Dawson a paper which showed that the profits of the trip had amounted to $428.55.

"Well, well, well!" said Mr. Dawson, after carefully reading and re-reading this statement of account. "That is so far ahead of anything that I dreamed of that it makes me feel that I made a mistake in not going into the bug business instead of iron manufacture. Well, the sooner you fit out and start on your next trip, the sooner you will be rich men, I suppose."

"We cannot always expect to do so well as this," the Doctor replied. "Just now there happen to be few collectors out, and several of the museums had cash on hand to buy collections with; then, too, we were fortunate in doing well in so slightly explored a territory as Haiti."

"At any rate, you will have a very nice balance to draw against, even if you make a loss this time."

"It seems to us," said Ned, who had been talking the matter over with Harry, "that some of this balance ought to belong to the Doctor, who worked hardest of any; I think half ought to be his."

"Well said, my boy," Mr. Dawson replied. "So it ought!"

"No, I could not agree to that," said the Doctor. "Let it all stand in one sum now; then, when our partnership is finally dissolved, if you think best, I will agree to take one-third, but no more."

"All right, that's agreed to; and it is very fair," Mr. Dawson said. "And as all of it is now settled, I suppose you will soon be drawing on me for cash for the next expedition."

"Yes, we hope to get off in two weeks from now; don't we, boys?"

"Yes, sir; and then: 'Ho! for the Spanish Main!'" said Harry.

"And 'Hurrah! for the lands of everlasting spring!'" sang Ned.

www.ingramcontent.com/pod-product-compliance
Lightning Source LLC
Chambersburg PA
CBHW032103230426
43672CB00009B/1625